ALEXAN

Beyond the Secret

the definitive unauthorized guide to *The Secret*

disinformation®

Published by:
The Disinformation Company Ltd.
163 Third Avenue, Suite 108
New York, NY 10003
Tel.: +1.212.691.1605
Fax: +1.212.691.1606
www.disinfo.com

Library of Congress Control Number: 2007938122

ISBN: 978-1932857-93-1

Cover & text design: Greg Stadnyk
Managing editor: Ralph Bernardo

Printed in USA

Distributed in USA and Canada by:
Consortium Book Sales and Distribution
Toll Free: +1.800.283.3572
Fax: +1.612.746.2606
www.cbsd.com

disinformation®

For Maria Beatriz Benetti Bensinger

ACKNOWLEDGEMENTS

I am most grateful to Gary Baddeley for giving me the opportunity to rummage around the world of self-help. It's been very confronting and terrifying at times but the "only way out is through," as they say!

I would also like to thank the producers of the film phenomenon, *The Secret*, Rhonda Byrne, Paul Harrington and Bob Rainone, who have served to remind so many of us of what is humanly possible.

Most of all, I wish to express my gratitude to each one of the outstanding people who were interviewed in the film, especially Bill Harris and Bob Doyle, who were kind enough to personally help me sort out some important ideas in certain chapters of this book. I would also like to thank Ken Wilber's Integral Institute, The Divine College of Metaphysics, Terry Melanson and William Bloom for giving me permission to reproduce large tracts of their excellent material. A big thanks goes to Wallace D. Wattles, the entire text of whose remarkable little book, *The Science of Getting Rich* is appended to the end of this one.

I would also like to thank some other gifted teachers, not interviewed for *The Secret* but who are nonetheless powerhouses in today's world of strategic philosophers, who inspire us to breathe joy and accomplishment into all aspects of our everyday lives. These people include Ken Wilber, Stewart & Joan Emery, Sonia Powers, Janet Attwood, Scott deMoulin & Dallyce Brisbin, Jay Conrad Levinson, Chet Holmes, Jim Bunch, Gene McNaughton and especially Sydney Cresci and her heavenly Make a Change Personal Life Journey® cruise. Were the commitment to integrity, love and greatness demonstrated by these people the standard by which all human beings would conduct themselves, every corner of planet Earth would be a paradise.

I also want to thank my personal champions: Demian Lichtenstein, for keeping the dream alive, Dave Sokolin, for exhibiting greatness nonstop and to my giant cherub, Glen Baietti, for putting up with me—and for putting a roof over my head.

TABLE OF CONTENTS

FOREWORD

"As evidenced by its incredible popularity, there are millions of people who are starving for something other than traditional religion or modern science in their search for meaning."

Ken Wilber's *Integral Naked* newsletter

The Secret pushes your hottest buttons: your core values, what constitutes success for you—and are you anywhere near achieving whatever you think is success? Do you feel connected to a "higher power"? Is there really an easy way to integrate your job, family, friends and community into creating a life that matters?

We Americans take the attainment of our success very seriously; when confronted with our relative achievement or lack thereof, that ever-present underlying anxiety leaps to center stage. Promising an easy solution to "having it all," *The Secret* became one of the bestselling books of 2007 (only the new *Harry Potter* sold more copies).

The book you hold in your hands seeks to provide the reader with a deeper background and context for the swirl of ideas presented by Rhonda Byrne and the twenty-odd "teachers" who created *The Secret*. There is something of a misperception that the teachers featured in the film and in the book present a unified method for achieving life goals—but this is hardly the case. Some teachers are corporate, others are more science- and tech-oriented, while at least one brazenly embraces the occult.

In a way that is not possible within the 90-minute format of a feature film, this book delves more deeply into the array of techniques and programs devised by the main speakers introduced in *The Secret*, geared for people who would like to know more about their teachings but who may not have the time or the money to personally investigate them all.

The foundation of most of the presenters' teachings can be traced to the New Thought movement that flourished in the United States from the mid-19th Century through the mid-20th Century and has always been characterized by its diversity and competing branches.

The Secret is the first commercial feature film presentation of New Thought, a movement which seemingly became sidetracked by the tumult of the 1960s and later either splintered off into middling self-help modalities or else became conflated with its woollier sibling, the New Age movement.

Sometime in the wake of 9/11 and during the course of "Operation Iraqi Freedom," I began to notice that marketing gurus had replaced the Pleiadian channelers in the Whole Life Expo circuit, which was probably a good thing. The relevance of extraterrestrials had apparently gotten lost in the brutal reality of war, not to mention the equally grisly metastasis of an aggressive tabloid industry, where celebrities provide a more dependable and glitzy supply of weirdness than the odd conspiracy theorist. Moreover, celebrities put a mirror up to our cultural notions of "success" and force the public to question its meaning (all the more reason why the public has become so ripe for *The Secret*).

The reader can therefore take comfort that there will be no Pleiadians or Zeta Reticuli appearing anywhere in this book—or any gossip about tabloid celebrities, for that matter. However, it is true that a major inspiration for *The Secret* does involve the trance-channeled messages of a group consciousness calling itself "Abraham" that speaks through a woman named Esther Hicks.

One of the controversies surrounding *The Secret* is that Esther Hicks was cut out of the original film and that the Hicks-free version is what is now for sale. Because Abraham's "Law of Attraction" remains the central theme of the film, I thought it important to include the very interesting story of "Abraham-Hicks" in this book.

There has also been some controversy about what has been described as the "relentless materialism" espoused by some of the speakers in *The Secret* and I must admit that some of the comments made in the film did initially strike me as rather fiendish. But limited-edition BMWs are not the only thing *The Secret* is about and I advise the reader to not throw the baby out with the bathwater.

There is unquestionably something of real value in *The Secret*: You. There exists a very real possibility of your living the life of your dreams. If you are willing to commit yourself to this, there are twenty-odd ways presented in this book to help you achieve it.

I encourage those whose curiosity is piqued by what they find here to investigate the teachers' books, films and websites further and, ideally, to live happier, healthier lives. For the most part, over the course of studying them, I have been inspired by the life work and the achievements of the people interviewed in *The Secret*.

At the time of this writing, I have no affiliation with the filmmakers, although I have been in touch with some of the people featured in *The Secret*.

Finally, this book intends to shed some light on the technological and economic forces at work behind the film's production, which helped fuel its success, and also to address the stark divergence of responses *The Secret* has received by different communities around the world.

Alexandra Bruce

1

THE BUSINESS END OF *THE SECRET*

> "Rhonda just wants to bring
> happiness to everybody."

Irene Izon,
Mother of Rhonda Byrne

By now, it's not hyperbole to describe *The Secret* as the most successful self-help film and book, ever. The book alone significantly raised the profits of entertainment colossus Viacom, selling at least four times more than any other book in the United States during the first half of 2007.

How did this largely derivative book, little more than a transcript of an underground film (which itself could, uncharitably, be described as a feature-length infomercial), have outsold new books by the likes of fiction giants James Patterson and Jodi Picoult, a celebrity memoir by Sidney Poitier and even the diet book du jour, *You On A Diet*?

The Secret Movie

Most credit really has to go to the film's creator, 55-year-old Australian reality television producer Rhonda Byrne. The official website describes the project's genesis as follows:

> ...on that spring day in 2004, when a small, old book called *The Science of Getting Rich* was put into her hands...Rhonda's whole life suddenly pulled into spectacular focus, she knew exactly what her mission was to become. She was going to take this knowledge to the world. She was going to make a movie to carry joy to every corner of the Earth. And so the great journey that was *The Secret* began...

> One of Rhonda's initial intentions for the creation of the show was that [she] would use *The Secret* to make *The Secret*...that it would be an effortless, joyful journey as they attracted everything and everyone that was needed to fulfill the vision. And right when the company was ready to begin production, as if by magic, the perfect people to make *The Secret* began to appear...

> The day Prime Time Productions arrived in the United States to film the living masters of *The Secret*, they only had one interview lined up. But they brought with them an entire crew, and the firm intention that they would film every person they needed for

the show. And in a matter of a few weeks, the team filmed fifty-two "teachers" of *The Secret*. Wherever the team went, more and more amazing teachers would emerge—great writers, leaders, philosophers, doctors, and scientists. These teachers created the foundation for *The Secret*.[1]

Their project has certainly led a charmed life. After all, it's not every $3 million film that starts out as a self-marketed Internet download and ends up buoying the share price of a multi-billion dollar entertainment conglomerate.

The original version of the movie was first made available on March 26, 2006 via the producers' slick website at www.thesecret.tv. For a fee of $4.95, visitors to the site could download the movie using sophisticated technology from a company called Vividas. The producers also sold DVDs from the website for $34.95, although they were usually discounted by $5. Regardless of the selling price, with no wholesale or retail intermediaries, the profit margins were extraordinarily high and it didn't take long for the film to recoup the $3 million production cost.

Byrne went on to tap former IBM salesman and Internet/telecommunications executive Robert Rainone as the US-based CEO of her new company, TS Productions LLC. They took advantage of Amazon.com's willingness to distribute and sell DVDs from single-title producers (something hardly any traditional video retailers would consider) and began selling the DVD via Amazon in October 2006, where sales immediately shot up despite minimal promotion beyond word-of-mouth.

The Secret Society

The key here is *who's* words and mouths. Whether by dint of the Law of Attraction or a brilliant, calculated move on Rhonda's part, most of the interviews that appear in *The Secret* were filmed at a biannual meeting of the Transformational Leadership Council (TLC). This proved to be fateful, indeed.

The TLC is a members-only group of self-help luminaries founded by *Chicken Soup for the Soul* author Jack Canfield, who has become something of a Godfather in the self-help industry. Like Canfield, many of the TLC's members are marketing geniuses who have successful careers as consultants to Fortune 500 companies. The aggregate sales power of all the people interviewed in *The Secret* is mammoth and each was able to mobilize his or her own network in support of the film, catapulting Rhonda into the stratosphere of super-success.

By May 2007, Rhonda was in *Time* magazine's "100 People Who Shape Our World," a list from which the news media at the time made great hay out of the fact that President George W. Bush was conspicuously absent. It was Jack Canfield himself who wrote Rhonda's entry in *Time*'s story:

...I first met Rhonda Byrne in July 2005, when she asked if she could bring her film crew to a meeting of the Transformational Leadership Council and interview our members for a movie she was creating called *The Secret*. For four days she and her crew filmed during the day and socialized with us at night. I was struck by her energy. She seemed to be in a constant state of bliss, of childlike wonder.

I am often asked why *The Secret* has been such a phenomenon—more than 2 million DVDs sold in a year and almost 4 million books in less than six months. It is primarily because Byrne's love and joy permeate every frame and every page. Her intention was pure and simple—to uplift as much of humanity as she could reach, and so far she has reached millions. And I believe she has only just begun.[2]

The Secret Religion

Besides high membership in the TLC, most of the speakers who appear in *The Secret* have been regulars on the New Thought/Unity Church circuit for years and they continue to speak regularly at Unity Churches all over America.

The principles espoused in *The Secret* are largely those of the Unity Church, the main New Thought denomination, much admired by Oprah Winfrey. Founded in

1889 by American husband and wife team Charles and Myrtle Fillmore, it has a present-day following of some 2,000,000 adherents around the world.

Whereas the new age hit film *What the Bleep Do We Know!?* was primarily affiliated with and supported by the Ramtha School of Enlightenment, *The Secret* has enjoyed a similar relationship with the larger and arguably more mainstream Unity Church, whose members have been instrumental in this film's promotion, at a grassroots level.

Both films have also benefited from the marketing advice of the Spiritual Cinema Circle and by the recruitment of the Transcendental Meditation™ movement. My guess is that for any similarly themed independent film to achieve the same level of success as *The Secret* and *What the Bleep Do We Know!?*, it would have to have similar alliances in place, in addition to a handful of unstoppable guerrilla marketing powerhouses, on a mission to outsell *The Secret*.

The Secret Technology

Everything about the success of the film, from its low production cost to its marketing and distribution, can pretty much be attributed to the disintermediation of the entertainment business. With affordable digital cameras and editing equipment, cheap website hosting, Internet video-on-demand, and direct-to-consumer order fulfillment from retail aggregators like Amazon.com,

Byrne and Rainone were able to bypass all of the traditional gatekeepers that might have been skeptical of their vision.

"Might" is probably generous. The recent success of *What The Bleep Do We Know?!*[3] notwithstanding, it's fairly safe to say that no movie studio or established home video distributor would have bankrolled the marketing and distribution of *The Secret*, let alone its production. It's also a safe bet that TS Productions won't be relying on Hollywood to finance or distribute its next projects. According to *Time* magazine, Byrne started shooting a sequel in January 2007 for release later in the year, quoting Rainone as saying that "it will explore 'the next step, the next level' in the process of achieving one's life goals."[4] Rainone also endorsed the video-on-demand technology provided by Vividas, saying "[i]t is a great way to launch a film and we plan to embrace it again with our future releases."[5]

The Secret Book

In July 2006, a book deal was made with Beyond Words, the publishers of Masaru Emoto's *Hidden Messages of Water* books, made popular by their featuring role in *What The Bleep Do We Know?!* "People are finding out about [*The Secret*] from other people," said Beyond Words publisher Cynthia Black, who heard about the DVD during a dinner conversation in Portland, Oregon, with one of the teachers featured in the movie.[6]

Whether consciously or not, Byrne and Rainone made a good choice by signing with Beyond Words. Black had recently entered into a deal with Viacom's Simon & Schuster publishing arm, via the Atria Books imprint. Judith Curr, Atria's publisher, was immediately enthusiastic, and they rushed a book version of *The Secret* into stores by November 2006. It was the combination of Beyond Words' New Age sensibilities and Atria's major publisher cash and clout that enabled the ensuing blockbuster success of the book.

According to Atria's Curr:

> "We never would have been able to have this book without Beyond Words, but Beyond Words would never have been able to publish this book…because the biggest problem that small presses have is that they can't fund their success…There's no way a small press is going to be able to order a 2 million-copy reprint, or even a 100,000-copy one, and then have the resources that you need to manage such a project."[7]

The book hit store shelves before Thanksgiving 2006, selling well enough to top New Age charts almost immediately but not in numbers sufficient to break onto cross-genre bestseller lists.

Until February 2007.

Oprah Winfrey, still the undisputed heavyweight champion of daytime television in the United States, invited Byrne and some of the teachers featured in *The Secret* to be on her show on February 8th. So successful was the appearance that a second show was scheduled a week later on February 16th.

The rest, as they say, is history. The book immediately shot to the top of every bestseller list for which it was eligible. Booksellers scrambled to try to find copies, taking orders from customers without any idea of when they might be able to fill them. This is a rare instance of a book spun off from a movie that far eclipsed the success of the movie in sales. And the movie itself had done (and continues to do) very well.

The Secret was brilliantly launched and quickly became a sales phenomenon of which the mainstream media took note. It would probably be easier to list by omission which newspapers, magazines, television talk shows and websites did not feature *The Secret*.

A Hickup (Sic)

As with life in general, the production of *The Secret* wasn't always as "joyful" of a "journey" as Rhonda might have liked. While she and her team did, indeed, interview some of the leading self-help and motivational speakers and authors working today, they had less luck with perhaps the most important of the teachers interviewed for the film.

The Secret had become such a success story that even the stodgiest, most august newspapers and magazines could not avoid devoting miles of column inches to debate the effectiveness of these New Age-sounding teachings, but in February 2007, the *New York Times* went a bit beyond its usual level of inquisitiveness and revealed that, "... behind the success of *The Secret* is a seamier story about the origins of the film. It involves big money and what some participants say are the broken promises of Ms. Byrne. The star of the first version of the movie, released in March last year, demanded to be cut out of the current version, which has been on the market since October 1."[8]

The author of the *Times* article, Allen Salkin, went on to describe how Esther Hicks had been promised 10% of the DVD revenues and various approvals over her portrayal. According to Salkin, Hicks and her husband, Jerry, were never happy with the film and eventually negotiations with the producers stalled (but not before the Hicks had earned $500,000). Ultimately, Hicks was edited out of a new version of the film, leaving the producers with a bigger share of the millions in royalties yet to come, which would have previously been payable to Hicks.

> In a backhanded compliment Ms. Hicks said, "I've got to give Rhonda credit," adding that her former collaborator has shown a monomaniacal dedication to the law of attraction. "I've never seen anybody do that like she's doing it," Ms. Hicks said. "And never mind honesty, and never mind doing what you said

you were going to do, and never mind anything. Just stay in alignment."[9]

Hicks and husband Jerry wrote a letter to friends setting out their version of events, stating:

> Eventually we received an email from the producer of *The Secret* lovingly explaining...that the contract that we had all agreed upon and signed was no longer sufficient for their further distribution of the project in the areas they were now seeking...and that it would be necessary for us (Jerry and Esther) to relinquish our intellectual property rights in these areas forever and redo our contract or they would have to reluctantly edit us out...after conferring with our publisher, and then our intellectual property rights attorney, and finally with Abraham, allowing them to edit us out was the path of least resistance...

> It is our desire that, rather than being upset that our part of *The Secret* will be omitted in future offerings of it, that instead you enjoy the original Abraham version, as it is, at this time, and that you look forward to what other incredible things these talented people may bring to you. These are people who clearly care about the planet, who want to be of value, and who, in our opinion, are of tremendous value.

> Financially speaking, we have been very well paid for our participation with this project...which has

amounted to a staggering amount of money. And if money were the most important factor, we assure you, we would have found some way of staying involved.[10]

The original version of the film with Esther Hicks can still be found on eBay and elsewhere on the Internet, but it's not the one that most of the millions of people who have bought copies of *The Secret* have in their possession.

The Hicks flap is probably the most obvious problem faced by Byrne, and one that she evidently overcame with aplomb. The next major problem was the kind that every publisher dreams of having: running out of stock while demand for the book was at its peak. For several weeks in February and March 2007 the book was not to be found in bookstores or even on Internet bookselling powerhouse Amazon.com, which usually listed it as available in 4–6 weeks. Judith Curr and her colleagues scrambled to print and ship more books, eventually setting a record for the largest reprint in Simon & Schuster's venerable history.

The shortage seemed only to fuel the fire of interest in all things "Secret"...

2

THE NEW THOUGHT MOVEMENT

"My greatest insights into The Secret... came from the teachings of Robert Collier, Prentice Mulford, Charles Haanel, and Michael Beckwith."

Rhonda Byrne

Producer

Like some people, I had misgivings about the presentaion of *The Secret*. At a time of "Operation Iraqi Freedom," genocide in Africa, global warming and celebrity meltdowns, *The Secret*'s message of visualizing your skinny body and attracting your brand new BMW seemed to me pathologically narcissistic if not almost criminal in its degeneracy.

Critics of *The Secret* have complained about the "relentless materialism"[1] espoused in the DVD and book. If *The Secret* is "spiritual," they ask, what are all these "wealth coaches" doing on this show?

The answer lies in the book that initially inspired the creation of *The Secret*, Wallace D. Wattles' *The Science of Getting Rich*. This book was expressly "intended for the men and women whose most pressing need is for money; who wish to get rich first, and philosophize afterward." In other words, Wattles' book was written for people who were desperate.

This was Rhonda's case, when the book landed in her hands. Lo and behold, she was a multi-millionaire within two years. Likewise, the film she made spoke to the denizens of the middle- and lower middle classes; people despairing over their credit card bills and dreaming of an escape from their financial enslavement. It's easy to see why dyed-in-the-wool cynics and those with big bank accounts would be the least likely to find any solace in the ideas presented in *The Secret*.

Wallace D. Wattles & *The Science of Getting Rich*

It wasn't until nearly a year after the film's release that I finally read the tiny little book, which Rhonda credits for setting her off on her great adventure, *The Science of Getting Rich* by Wallace D. Wattles. Its laser-like prose had a similarly electrifying impact on me, prompting me to dispose of the nagging cynicism that I'd had towards *The Secret* and inspiring in me a newfound interest in a fascinating episode in American history, known as the New Thought movement.

The Science of Getting Rich is so extraordinary that it has been reproduced in its entirety at the back of this book. Contrary to what the title suggests, it is not a "get-rich-quick" book and it contains virtually no hard financial or business advice. It is an elegant and concise manual about developing and sustaining a state of mind, which Wattles' calls "a Certain Way." His view, novel at the time, was that, "To live fully in soul, man must have love; and love is denied expression by poverty...It is the desire of God that you should get rich."

Wattles' main influences were philosophers Ralph Waldo Emerson and Georg Hegel, both of whom were heavily influenced by ancient Hindu and Buddhist texts, which were just then becoming more available in Western languages. The foundation of these religious philosophies is the concept of monism. In Wattles' words:

> The monistic theory of the universe is the theory that One is All, and that All is One; That one Substance manifests itself as the seeming many elements of the material world—is of Hindu origin, and has been gradually winning its way into the thought of the western world for two hundred years. It is the foundation of all the Oriental philosophies, and of those of Descartes, Spinoza, Leibnitz, Schopenhauer, Hegel, and Emerson.[2]

In 17th Century Europe, the "All is One" concept was as heretical to Christianity, Judaism and Islam as it is today and in 1656 the celebrated Dutch philosopher Spinoza was excommunicated from his Orthodox Jewish congregation because of the monistic expressions in his writings.

Thanks to the First Amendment of the US Constitution in 1787, Wattles had more freedom to synthesize his compelling blend of Eastern monism and American pragmatism; a fusion which remains as appealing as ever to the silent majority of the people around the world who are not hard line fundamentalists.

However, like Spinoza before him, Wattles was relieved from his position as a pastor of his Methodist Church due to his preaching of values which he ardently believed to be in alignment with Christianity, but which were evidently overruled as un-Christian by the local clergy.

Wattles' book *The Science of Getting Rich* is considered to be one of the classics of the New Thought movement and his overall philosophy, as expressed in the other books he wrote, including *A New Jesus, How To Be A Genius: The Science of Being Great, How to Energize Your Marriage, The New Science of Living and Healing, Lessons in Constructive Science: The Personal Power Course,* all show Wattles to be a model exponent of the New Thought movement which was burgeoning all around him, particularly in the Northeastern and Midwestern United States during his time.

Chronology of the New Thought Movement

The New Thought movement, which swept America starting in the mid-1800s through the mid-1900s, was an outgrowth of the Age of Enlightenment, also called the Age of Reason, which swept across much of Europe during the 1700s and during which time great advances in logic, science and law eventually culminated in the creation of the United States of America.

Many of the people Rhonda Byrne cites as "past teachers of The Secret" were instrumental players in the New Thought movement. The following is a timeline of the movement and its movers and shakers constructed by historical researcher Terry Melanson, which I've redacted slightly. Emphases are mine:

> **The New Age Movement** is generally traced back to the teachings of Theosophy and **Madame Helena Blavatsky (1831–1891).** In a similar manner, **Phineas Parkhurst Quimby (1802–1866)** laid the foundation for what became known as the **New Thought Movement**...Though less well-known, yet equally as diverse, New Thought has just as many branches and competing systems...
>
> **1838, Phineas P. Quimby** takes up the practice of mesmerism (mesmeric sleep or hypnotism), after attending a lecture in Belfast, Maine by a traveling

French physician/mesmerist, Dr. Collyer.

After a few experiments on willing subjects, Quimby happens upon a most suggestive young man, one Lucius Burkmar. Quimby soon realized that Burkmar, while in a trance, could diagnose disease and prescribe remedies. They traveled throughout New England and gave their own exhibitions—the mesmeric faith-healer and his talented clairvoyant.

Looking for an explanation to Burkmar's success—and not content with the standard mesmeric theory that magnetic fluid was the causative agent—Quimby theorized that healing occurred through the sheer power of the mind. Quimby would say, "Some believe in various remedies, and others believe that the spirits of the dead prescribe. I have no confidence in the virtue of either. I know that cures have been made in these ways. I do not deny them. But the principle on which they are done is the question to solve; for the disease can be cured, with or without medicine, on but one principle."

According to James Webb, "between 1852 and 1855," Quimby wrote, "I then became a medium myself." His own method of healing entailed retaining his own consciousness. "Now when I sit down by a diseased person I see the spiritual form of a vapor surrounding their bodies," Quimby had said. After inducing the patient to tell him where their trouble began, the cure was realized by Quimby's spirit governing their own; consisting "in bringing the spirit of his patient away from the place where the cause of illness occurred." (*The Occult Underground*, p. 122)

Thus, the Quimby system of mental healing of illness was born.

1862, After suffering chronic illness and dabbling in homeopathy and alternative healing, **Mary Baker Eddy (1821–1910)** turns to Phineas Quimby for treatment. Julius A. Dresser said that when Eddy "became a patient of Quimby, she at once took an interest in his theory, and imbibed his explanations of truth rapidly."

1866, After a fall on the sidewalk caused her to seek her own cure, Mary Baker Eddy says she "discovered the Science of Divine Metaphysical Healing, which I afterward named **Christian Science**." In reality, this "scientific certainty that all causation was Mind, and every effect a mental phenomenon," was based upon her own under-standing of the healing principles of Quimby.

1875, The foundational doctrine of the Christian Science movement, Eddy's *Science and Health* is published.

1879, Eddy founds **The First Church of Christ, Scientist** in Boston, Massachusetts.

1883, *The Christian Science Journal* is created by Eddy.

1885, Emma Curtis Hopkins (1849–1925) becomes an independent Christian Science practitioner after a falling out with Eddy's organization. Dubbed the "teacher of teachers," Hopkins would go on to influence and indoctrinate most of the early influential purveyors of New Thought. **Her students included** Emma Fox, **Myrtle and Charles Fillmore**, Ernest Holmes and Francis Lord. By 1887, Hopkins had "taught six hundred students" and had in operation seventeen branches of the Hopkins Metaphysical Association. (See Deidre Michell, "New Thinking, New Thought, New Age: The Theology and Influence of Emma Curtis Hopkins (1849–1925)," *Counterpoints*, Vol. 2, No. 1, July 2002)

Hopkins' own inspiration ran the gamut from Plotinus, Porphyry, and Spinoza, to the Zend-Avesta and alchemist Cornelius Agrippa. She promulgated aphorisms and affirmations such as "there is no evil"; "there is no matter"; "there is no sin, sickness or death"; and "my Good is my God." Combining 19th century feminism with New Thought Christian Science, Hopkins ordained ministers (mostly women) as "special messengers of 'the new era of the Holy Mother Spirit'" (Michell, op. cit.).

1889, The Unity Church (Unity, or Unity School of Christianity) is founded by Charles Fillmore

(1854–1948) and Myrtle Fillmore (1845–1931) in Kansas City, Missouri.

Besides New Thought and a metaphysical interpretation of the Bible, "Unity drew on Hinduism, Buddhism, Theosophy, and Rosicrucianism," declares Arthur Goldwag. Confirming Unity's syncretism, Charles Fillmore had said, "We have studied many isms, many cults...We have borrowed the best from all religions...Unity is the Truth that is taught in all religions, simplified...so that anyone can understand and apply it."

Unity as whole is the most powerful conduit for the dissemination of New Thought metaphysics, representing hundreds of affiliate churches, organizations, offshoots and perhaps millions of followers. Purportedly, Oprah Winfrey is a member. (At the very least, she is and has been, the promoter of many prominent members—most recently those involved with *The Secret*).

1895, In Boston, the **Metaphysical Club** is formed. Up until that time, this represented the "chief event in the history of New Thought"; bringing together "some of the leaders of the mental-science period" and those "active in the Church of the Divine Unity and The Mental Healing Monthly."

1898, *Nautilus,* the most widely read New Thought

periodical, is created by Elizabeth Towne. It was published for over 50 years, "sold extensively on the newsstands, has taken the place of many of the earlier magazines, and is typical of the New Thought in its most popular and prosperous form."

1899, The Metaphysical Club organizes a conference in Boston for those with a "deep interest in the new movement to establish a world-wide unity and cooperation along the lines of the so-called 'New Thought.'" In turn, an International **Metaphysical League** was organized at this conference. During its second session in 1900 a revised constitution was adopted, the purpose of which was:

> "To establish unity and cooperation of thought and action among individuals and organizations throughout the world devoted to the Science of Mind and of Being, and to bring them, so far as possible, under one name and organization; to promote interest in and the practice of a true spiritual philosophy of life; to develop the highest self-culture through right thinking, as a means of bringing one's loftiest ideals into present realization; to stimulate faith in and the study of the highest nature of man, in its relation to health, happiness, and progress; to teach the universal Fatherhood and Motherhood of God and the all-inclusive Brotherhood of Man; that One Life is immanent in the universe, and is both

Centre and Circumference of all things visible and invisible, and that the Intelligence is above all and in all; and that from this Infinite Life and Intelligence proceed all Light, Love and Truth. These simple statements are in their nature tentative, and imply no limitations or boundaries to future progress and growth, as larger measures of light and truth shall be revealed."

1908, *The Christian Science Monitor* is founded by Mary Baker Eddy.

1912, Businessman, "thirty-second degree Mason and a Shriner," **Charles F. Haanel (1866–1949)** wrote his mind-power prosperity classic, *The Master Key System*. It sold over 200,000 copies [over] the next twenty years.

1914, The International New Thought Alliance is formed. Its purpose:

"To teach the infinitude of the Supreme One; the Divinity of Man and his Infinite possibilities through the creative power of constructive thinking and obedience to the voice of the Indwelling Presence, which is our source of Inspiration, Power, Health and Prosperity.

"Since its inception, the International New Thought Alliance has organized annual conferences, bringing together the great leaders of New Thought in the world, including representatives from Unity School, United Religious Science, Religious Science International, Divine Science, Association of Unity Churches, Universal Foundation for Better Living, Center for Spiritual Awareness, Unity Progressive Council, Association of Global New Thought, New Thought Network, University of Healing, as well as noted individuals..."

Its headquarters acts as a research institute. The Addington INTA Archives consists of books and booklets, magazines, pamphlets, correspondences, lectures, sermons, lessons and published articles dealing with all aspects relating to New Thought, the New Age and occultism. In addition to recognized New Thought authors, the Addington INTA Archives allows one to delve into the major writings of New Age pioneers Alice A. Bailey and Annie Besant; occultist William Wynn Westcott; Gurdjieff disciples J.G. Bennett, P.D. Ouspensky, Maurice Nicoll and G.I. Gurdjieff himself; Sri Aurobindo; Francis Bacon; Emanuel Swedenborg; Theosophists C.W. Leadbeater, J. Krishnamurti and H.P. Blavatsky; Edgar Cayce; Pierre Teilhard de Chardin; some of the *Seth* material channeled by Jane Roberts; a book by the Findhorn Community, *The Findhorn Garden* (on how they contacted and cooperated with "nature spirits and devas"); Freemason/occult philosopher Manly P. Hall; the Rosicrucian writings of Max Heindel;

H.S. Lewis, the founder of the Rosicrucian Order AMORC; New Agers, Barbara Marx Hubbard, Ruth Montgomery, and Luciferians John Randolph Price and David Spangler; Swedenborgian Helen Keller's *My Religion*; spirit medium JZ Knight (Ramtha's School of Enlightenment); and the *Book of Urantia*— among others.

1921, On the 100th anniversary of Mary Baker Eddy's birth, an exact replica of the Great Pyramid, made from a single piece of granite and weighing over 100 tons and 11 feet on each side, was carved and placed near the house where Eddy had been born, in New Hampshire. It was a gift from Freemasons. In the "Mary Baker Eddy Letter," December 25, 1997, we learn that when "the Board of Directors noted that too many Christian Scientists were visiting the grand granite marker at Bow...that marked Mary Baker Eddy's birthplace, they had it destroyed, dynamited to bits!"

Eddy's first husband, George Washington Glover, was a Mason, and "thereafter membership in the Masonic Order was the one single 'outside' affiliation that was allowed to church members by Mrs. Eddy."

Christian Science and Freemasonry have maintained a symbiotic relationship. Many of the first churches established around the United States had gathered in Masonic Temples. To this day one can find the headquarters for many Christian Science associations having an address corresponding to the local Masonic lodge...

1937, Napoleon Hill (1883–1970), a practitioner of Haanel's *The Master Key System*, publishes *Think and Grow Rich*. Hill's "Science of Success" was sometimes dubbed the "Carnegie Secret" or the "Carnegie Formula." He had had a longtime relationship with Andrew Carnegie, beginning with the latter commissioning him to interview the most successful, wealthy and famous people in the world.

Hill would later claim that he had been contacted by a visitor from another dimension. "I come from the Great School of Masters," the being had said. "I am one of the Council of Thirty-Three who serve the Great School and its initiates on the physical plane." According to Hill, his greatest secrets came from spirit guides known "as the Venerable Brotherhood of Ancient India, it is the great central reservoir of religious, philosophical, moral, physical, spiritual and psychical knowledge. Patiently this school strives to lift mankind from spiritual infancy to maturity of soul and final illumination." (See Dave Hunt, "The Classic Case of Napoleon Hill")

1952, Norman Vincent Peale (1898–1993) publishes *The Power of Positive Thinking*. The book became an instant bestseller, was "on the *New York*

Times' bestseller list for 186 consecutive weeks," and has sold over 7 million copies. A Christian preacher and a 33rd degree Freemason, Peale "and his chief disciple, Robert Schuller, kept New Thought alive within mainstream Christianity."

1974, A black female minister from the Unity School of Christianity, Dr. **Johnnie Coleman,** founds the **Universal Foundation for Better Living**, and in 1985, the **Christ Universal Temple** in Chicago. Oprah regular, Della Reese, the star of TV's *Touched by an Angel*, was ordained a minister by Universal Foundation for Better Living. Reese and Coleman together founded the Understanding Principles for Better Living Church.

1975, *A Course in Miracles* (ACIM), by Dr. Helen Schucman (1910–1981), is published. ACIM represents "the most successful channeled work of the late twentieth century." It has been embraced by New Thought and New Age teachers alike. Workshops and seminars espousing the principles of ACIM have become a staple of Unity and Religious Science.

Oprah Winfrey has been an ardent promoter of ACIM, mainly through the teachings of New Age/Unity feel-good guru **Marianne Williamson**, who's been a frequent guest.[3]

Alleged "Past Teachers of *The Secret*"

In addition to some of the names listed in the above chronology, Rhonda's book alleges that numerous celebrated figures, ranging from antiquity to the present were "past teachers of The Secret." These included Aristotle, Plato, Hermes Trismegistus, Buddha, Beethoven, Victor Hugo, Isaac Newton, Alexander Graham Bell, Thomas Edison, Henry Ford, Winston Churchill, Albert Einstein, Carl Jung, W. Clement Stone, Robert Collier, Thomas Troward, Dr. Martin Luther King, Jr. and Joseph Campbell.

While none of these men ever publicly propounded what Rhonda calls "The Secret," she is most likely alluding to the streams of monism and self-responsibility that are evident in all of these men's writings.

What is not generally known about many of these luminaries is that some were allegedly practitioners of alchemy, a philosophical and spiritual discipline that was considered to be a serious science in Europe up until the 16th Century.

The one name in Rhonda's list of "Past Teachers of The Secret" which leapt out at me was the mysterious "Hermes Trismegistus," the possible author of the equally mysterious "Emerald Tablet," and the alleged inventor of alchemy and Hermetic philosophy, as described on the *The Secret*'s website:

The Emerald Tablet is perceived as one of the most important historical documents known to mankind and is thousands of years old. Throughout history the question has been posed: was it written by a man or a god? Its author is ultimately unknown but it is speculated to be the mythical Greco-Egyptian deity Hermes Trismegistus—inventor of alchemy and Hermetic philosophy. Since ancient Egyptian times the Emerald Tablet has been translated by many of the world's greatest thinkers including Sir Isaac Newton and has been revered by alchemists, scientists and philosophers. It discusses the interconnectedness and oneness of all things and also the nature of the universe and creation. The Emerald Tablet is sometimes viewed as a guide to assist humans in understanding their relationship to the universe. The original tablet was lost around the 4th Century, having been concealed from religious zealots who were rampaging throughout the civilized world destroying artifacts. One theory holds that the tablet was buried in the sands of the Giza Plateau.[4]

I was surprised to discover in my research that Sir Isaac Newton actually wrote more about alchemy than he did about the things for which he later became famous. One of the alchemical texts found among his papers after he died was the abovementioned translation of the "Emerald Tablet."

In an early sequence of *The Secret* movie, the "Emerald Tablet" is seen being hurriedly transcribed and buried in the sand by an ancient Egyptian scribe, with soldiers in hot pursuit.

The oldest documented source of the "Emerald Tablet" was allegedly written around 800 ad by the Persian Sufi sheikh, Abd al-Qadir al-Jilani. That text supposedly hints at the recipe for alchemical gold and suggests how to set one's level of consciousness to a higher level.

Isaac Newton's Translation of the Emerald Tablet

1. Tis true without lying, certain & most true.

2. That which is below is like that which is above & that which is above is like that which is below to do the miracles of one only thing.

3. And as all things have been & arose from one by the meditation of one: so all things have their birth from this one thing by adaptation.

4. The Sun is its father, the moon its mother.

5. The wind hath carried it in its belly, the earth its nurse.

6. The father of all perfection in the whole world is here.

7. Its force or power is entire if it be converted into earth.

7a. Separate thou the earth from the fire, the subtle from the gross sweetly with great industry.

8. It ascends from the earth to the heaven & again it descends to the earth and receives the force of things superior & inferior.

9. By this means you shall have the glory of the whole world & thereby all obscurity shall fly from you.

10. Its force is above all force, for it vanquishes every subtle thing & penetrates every solid thing.

11a. So was the world created.

12. From this are & do come admirable adaptations where of the means (or process) is here in this.

13. Hence I am called Hermes Trismegist, having the three parts of the philosophy of the whole world.

14. That which I have said of the operation of the Sun is accomplished & ended.[5]

Clearly, one would need to be an initiate into the mysteries in order to understand the meaning of the wisdom above. The only verse that is unambiguous to me is number three, which proclaims the monistic view, "as all things have been & arose from one by the meditation of one: so all things have their birth from this one thing by adaptation."

It is beyond the scope of this book to expound any further on the vast and fascinating topic of Hermetic philosophy, of which alchemy is a part. However, its presence can be felt throughout *The Secret*, leading certain religious paranoids to suspect that the film and book are some kind of "Rosicrucian Conspiracy," a topic that I will discuss in slightly more detail later.

Prentice Mulford & *The White Cross Library*

Born in 1834, Prentice Mulford is considered to be an early pioneer of the New Thought movement. A visionary who made his living at odd jobs and as a writer for San Francisco newspapers, he lived as a hermit towards the end of life, during which time he wrote his six-volume series of essays called *The White Cross Library*.

He was interested in mental and spiritual phenomena and he reportedly practiced telepathy. His dreamlike essays were inspired mostly by his contact with nature. He wrote, "In the spiritual life every person is his or her own discoverer, and you need not grieve if your discoveries are not believed in by others. It is your business to push on, find more and increase your own individual happiness."[6]

Charles Haanel &
The Master Key System

Charles Haanel was a successful industrialist in the early 20th Century and he is best known today as the author of *The Master Key System*, which teaches the principles, causes, effects, and laws that underlie all attainment and success. Again, we see a monistic, Hindu current in his views, as seen throughout New Thought and Unity Church literature.

Haanel received several college degrees over the course of his life, including a Medical Doctorate from the Universal College of Dupleix, in India and a degree in Metaphysics from the College of Divine Metaphysics, in California.

It is worthwhile to read the definition of "Metaphysical Law" on the College of Divine Metaphysics' website because it pretty well encapsulates the worldview of all of the teachers of *The Secret*. Essentially, this definition of "Metaphysical Law" *is* "The Secret":

Metaphysical Law

Man's existence on this earth plane is not dependent upon material things, but is dependent upon metaphysical law. Progress and inventions are the result of thought. Some claim that progress is the outgrowth of the soul, but soul is mind; therefore, creative thought must precede the translation of ecstatic feeling into fine art or other creations.

The same Universal Mind which inspires one person to write beautiful poems leads another to outstanding success in business or finance. All wisdom and power reside in Universal Mind, and through his inner consciousness, each individual takes from the universal that with which his individual mind correlates, that which is nearest like what he is in thought and feeling.

In other words, we tune in on our own wave length. No mistake is made; that which comes to us out of the universal comes because we attract it with our thoughts and feelings.

Out of this deeper phase of mind comes all inspiration, whether it leads to the writing of a powerful book, the painting of an exquisite picture, the launching of a great invention, or the victory in a right and just cause. All of man's marvelous and remarkable achievements are simply the outpouring of thought from the inexhaustible fountainhead of Universal Mind.[7]

Urban legends circulate that an unspecified "church" banned Haanel's book in 1933, after which it went out of print, with the original copies trading furiously on the rare book market. This is supposedly how Bill Gates obtained his copy while he was still a student at Harvard. *The Master Key System* allegedly gave Gates the courage to drop out of college and to found Microsoft.

> It is Silicon Valley's secret that almost every entrepreneur who made a fortune in recent years did so by studying the words Mr. Haanel, penned over eighty years ago! Almost every millionaire and billionaire in the Valley read *The Master Key System* by Charles F. Haanel. Since this book was no longer in print until recently, copies of *The Master Key System* became a hot commodity in the Valley.[8]

Luckily, *The Master Key System* is now a public domain text that is available as a free download on the Internet.

Michael Beckwith & Agape

Michael Beckwith is the only living teacher who Rhonda credits most with her own personal transformation. He is the founder of the Agape International Spiritual Center in Los Angeles, CA and he describes himself as a "non-aligned trans-religious progressive." He participates on international panels with peacemakers and spiritual leaders, including His Holiness the Dalai Lama of Tibet, Dr. T. Ariyarante of Sri Lanka, and Arun Gandhi, grandson of Mohandas K. Gandhi.

Agape is described as "a trans-denominational spiritual

community whose doors are open to all seekers in search of authentic spirituality, personal transformation and selfless service to humankind."[9]

Beckwith is the author of *40-Day Mind Fast Soul Feast*, *A Manifesto of Peace*, and *Living from the Overflow* and he travels frequently to speak at Unity and other affiliated churches across the country, leading groups in his "Visioning Process."

> Visioning is a process by which we train ourselves to be able to hear, feel, see, and catch God's plan for our life or for any particular project we're working on. It differs from visualization in that we are allowing God's idea to come forth rather than attempting to create specific things that we want to manifest. There are conscious steps of centering, silence, gratitude and more...[10]

I have been most lucky to attend a high-energy Agape service given by Beckwith in Los Angeles. His talk about "pet peeves" was riotously funny, unfathomably deep and absolutely brilliant. The gist of the talk was that people fixate on dumb little things that get in the way of their happiness and of their spiritual insight and the more they allow themselves to be distracted and annoyed, those things will show up to bug them, all the more.

Beckwith also had some words for churchgoers who were more concerned about *how* they worshipped, rather than the *act* of worshipping, itself. He criticized those who worshipped their particular *form of worship* more than they worshipped God, Himself.

At the time, I was unaware of any friction between Agape and any other Christian church but after researching for this book, I can now see that these comments were clearly in response to what certain fundamentalists have said about Beckwith and his church.

For my part, Beckwith's Agape service was the most uplifting experience that I've ever had in a church or "spiritual" environment. The choir was incredible! If you live in LA or if you're just visiting town and happen to be there on a Sunday, the amazing opportunity of attending Beckwith's powerful talk, along with communing with a group of such loving, wonderful people is a phenomenal event that I would unreservedly recommend to anyone!

3

ABRAHAM & THE LAW OF ATTRACTION

"You're picky about the car you drive.

You're picky about what you wear.

You're picky about what
you put in your mouth.

We want you to be pickier
about what you think."

Abraham-Hicks

Jerry Hicks and his wife Esther grew up in typical Christian households in the Western United States. Jerry describes himself as a man who has been on a quest for truth his whole life. In his early twenties, he dabbled with a ouija board with some friends and found that he was actually able to communicate with something "on the other end." The ouija board instructed him to read everything he could get his hands on about

Albert Schweitzer. Eventually, however, the ouija board frightened his wife and he stopped using it.

Napoleon Hill & *Seth Speaks*

Next, Jerry read Napoleon Hill's *Think and Grow Rich*, which inspired him to start a company from which he and several others did grow rich. But there was a still a fundamental truth out there that eluded him and which he wanted more than anything to learn.

Then Jerry came into contact with the series of books published in the 1970s by Jane Roberts who channeled a being who called himself "Seth." Jerry found these books to be totally fascinating (as did I). Again, Esther was creeped-out by the idea of a disembodied entity speaking though the body of someone who was alive but once she realized that Seth's opinions of the vast array of non-physical personalities was akin to the way many embodied people regard each other, she began to relax. For example, Seth described some entities as "just plain dumb" but he had the profoundest respect for other beings. Esther's intuition told her that Seth's information "felt good" and that was the basis that she used to guide her life. Today, Esther credits her encounter with the Seth books for setting her off on her journey of channeling for large audiences.

Esther was so enthused by what she read in the first Seth

book that she became determined both to meet Jane Roberts personally and to read all of the other Seth books. Unfortunately, Roberts had just passed away. Soon, the couple encountered a psychic who taught them how to meditate, something that they had never done before. They began doing this for 15–30 minutes every day for several months, learning to clear their minds of what is known as "mind chatter."

Enter Abraham

The results of Esther's experiments were completely unexpected...she experienced a physically strong, "goose-bumpy" feeling in her body and the words within her mind were, "I am your spiritual guide, I am Abraham." Her hands were powerfully dragged towards the typewriter, causing considerable concern for both her and Jerry because of the degree of force.

For the next few months, Esther typed out Abraham's teachings for 15 minutes every day. Later, Abraham began to speak through her voice, in a slightly different accent from her own. Today, Esther says a brief farewell before going into a trance to "go get Abraham."

According to an MP3 audio recording[1] of Abraham available on the Abraham-Hicks website, the vocabulary and basic knowledge possessed by Esther is available to the Abraham collective, in order to better speak in the vernacular of American English, but the broader perspectives communicated by the non-physical collective consciousness called "Abraham" has no origin in Esther's mind.[2]

The first MP3 file begins by stating that this communication is an introduction of the non-physical to physical beings, something that both have wanted for a long, long time. Abraham goes on to explain that there are many non-physical beings around us and that there are many simple laws, which guide everything, physical and non-physical.

The goal of the Abraham collective is to open the passageway between the listeners' physical and non-physical aspects. Abraham describes one who is truly in joy with everything that it is happening on Earth as an "Allower." The Abraham collective wishes to help people identify and express their life purpose.

Abraham-Hicks: The Main Teachings

The key precepts of Abraham-Hicks are that human beings are "spirit incarnate," i.e., physical extensions of their non-physical aspects and fundamentally connected to All That Is. Abraham teaches that human beings have chosen to incarnate in their physical bodies for the purpose of experiencing joy, freedom, creativity and growth. Abraham teaches that our thoughts are very powerful and that it is best to manage our thoughts, lest we create unwanted circumstances. Anything we can imagine can be ours to be, to do or to have. We are choosing everything in our lives, whether we are aware of this or not, so it is important for us to become aware of what we are choosing. The Universe adores every single one of us and it is constantly guiding us on our chosen paths, so we can relax in the knowledge that "All is well." No one can limit anybody's thinking and there are no limits to the joyous journeys we can experience. Any action we take and any money we exchange should be a by-product of our focus on joy. It is possible to depart our bodies without pain or illness and we cannot truly die, as we are Everlasting Life. Our natural state is Foreverness.[3]

Again, we see the monist current, with the similarly optimistic, positive, worldview that we find in Unity teachings, with an additional "feel-good" instruction. To my knowledge the two groups were not previously affiliated but it appears that *The Secret* may have had the effect of putting them into contact, as their philosophies are not dissimilar.

The Law of Attraction

Abraham teaches that the Law of Attraction is the most important law of the universe and that virtually everything in your life is a reflection of your dominating thoughts.

You can harness the power of this law in a deliberate fashion, as opposed to by default. Setting your intention forth; visualizing and feeling its reality is a very powerful and effective process. This can be done with larger visions, as well as moment-to-moment, where you can "pre-pave" segments of your path, as the author of your life.

Abraham makes a key distinction between "allowance" and "tolerance." Allowance is crucial to the process of deliberate intention and creation, whereas tolerance is a condition of energetically binding yourself to that which you do not choose.

The Astonishing Power of Emotions

Jerry and Esther Hicks were so excited about the clarity and the practicality of the translated words of Abraham that they began sharing these with their close business associates. When these people began plying Abraham with meaningful personal questions regarding their finances, bodily conditions, and relationships, the Hickses decided that the time had come to take the show on the road, so that Abraham's teachings could be made available to the ever-widening circle of seekers.

Jerry and Esther have since published more than 600 Abraham-Hicks books, CDs, cassettes, DVDs, and videos, and they have been presenting open group interactive Art of Allowing™ workshops in up to 60 cities each year.

Their latest book, *The Astonishing Power of Emotions: Let Your Emotions Be Your Guide* teaches that human beings are "source energy" who are currently embodied in physical form. As people come forth in their physical bodies, they see a variety of things, all around them, which inspire a constant series of new preferences. Each of these new preferences, whether voiced or not, moves forth from a person like a "rocket of desire" into what Abraham calls a "vibrational escrow."

"Rockets of desire" emanate from people every day. When a person recognizes something that they don't want, a "rocket of desire" flows through that person and their broader, nonphysical aspect begins to resonate with the unwanted thing, becoming its vibrational equivalent. Typically, a duality exists within each person; two vibrational points of reference that are always playing off one another, 1) where they are right now vs. 2) where they would prefer to be.

What Abraham would have people asking themselves all day, every day is: "is the physical, mortal part of me, with all that I am thinking and doing a vibrational match to the larger vibrational part of me?"

Because if it *is* a vibrational match, then not only is it in that moment, a match to the larger part of the human being but also to the vibrational escrow that is there, where the larger part of the person is. In other words, the person is in alignment with their higher self.

The Astonishing Power of Emotions was written in response to the rush of people learning about the Law of Attraction through *The Secret* and the growing awareness among the populace that people do in some way create their own realities. However, Abraham says that most people don't understand *how* to create.

According to Abraham, the key to creating what you want is in understanding how you feel in the present, relative to how you would feel if you actually had what you wanted. Doing an exercise such as this would be a great way to get a handle on your thought processes and on how you create your reality.

The book outlines 33 examples of all kinds of things that might happen in someone's life. Abraham claims that as the reader explores the examples in the order in which they are given, by the time they've read through all 33 examples the reader will be attuned and be in vibrational alignment with what they truly want and be back into alignment with who they truly are.

> You have had access to the power that creates worlds for a very long time and you haven't known it. You've been dabbling in creating, in an action-oriented, many times upstream, mediocre way. When you begin to tune yourself to the energy of who it is you really are, then you begin to create, as you've intended.[4]

Overall, I enjoy listening to what Esther-Abraham says;

for the most part, the information is soothing and loving. I do not think it can do anybody harm, as long as long as they are of sound mind and body, but if "doing what feels good" is somebody's deleterious drug habit, then there could be problems with that person's following Abraham's teachings...

Mainstream Reaction to "Abraham"

It's amazing how little flak *The Secret* has received over having been largely inspired by messages coming from a disembodied group consciousness, calling itself "Abraham," that were "channeled" through a woman named Esther Hicks. I have seen virtually none of the ridicule leveled against Hicks' channeling activities of Abraham as I did in my investigation of JZ Knight's channeling of Ramtha.[5]

The unconventional means by which *The Secret*'s central material was obtained is rarely referred to and when it is, even by a mainstream publication like the *New York Times*, it is very matter-of-fact. This may be a product of the relatively sound, "feel good" nature of Abraham's messages, in contrast to the occasionally weird ramblings of Ramtha...

Perhaps one day, a science will be developed to map out the many unseen dimensions and worlds that have been described throughout history in countless civilizations. Until then, there will always be those who view such phenomena as "Abraham" as a hoax and a con of the highest order.

As much as I happen to appreciate Abraham's messages, I have no doubt that *The Secret*'s break from the association with the "woo-woo" factor of this disembodied group consciousness has only served to help increase the sales of the movie/book.

But while the parting of the ways may have helped increase sales of *The Secret*, Hicks is concerned that the true meaning of the Law of Attraction will be "destroyed" as a result:

> The Hickses have preached the law of attraction while traveling with Abraham for 21 years. Ms. Byrne's exposure to the notion is more recent [2004]...

> What the Hickses say bothers them most about the second version of *The Secret* is that those who watch it are not receiving enough explanation of the law or being told that its discovery was made by "vibrationally accessing broader intelligence," Ms. Hicks said.

> Bringing forth the voice of Abraham as she sat on a buttery leather seat in her motor home, speaking of herself in the third person, she said, "Esther's concern is that they will destroy this information because they do not really know it."[6]

4

THE *CHICKEN SOUP* POSSE

"The desire for riches is really the desire for a richer, fuller, and more abundant life; and that desire is praiseworthy."

Wallace D. Wattles
The Science of Getting Rich

In an era when a hedge fund manager's yearly salary can be $400 million while middle-class debtors are defaulting on their loans, it is understandable that wealth would be a national obsession and that *The Secret* would capture a lot of people's attention.

As it happens, many of the success coaches in this movie have endured extreme poverty and a surprising number of them have actually experienced homelessness. By dint of each one's indefatigable commitment to his or her vision, all have managed to make abundant lives for themselves and to thrive financially. Also, most of them are very quick to point out that financial wealth is just one aspect of an abundant life.

Jack Canfield: Uncanned

Probably one of the best known of *The Secret*'s teachers, Canfield is the creator, with co-author Mark Victor Hansen, of the ultra-successful *Chicken Soup for the Soul* series of books, hailed by *Time* magazine as "the publishing phenomenon of the decade." He claims to have over 115 titles and 100 million copies in print in over 47 languages and according to *USA Today*, Canfield and Hansen were the top-selling authors in the United States in 1997. Canfield has been a featured guest on more than 1,000 radio and television programs including *Oprah, 20/20, Inside Edition, The Today Show, Larry King Live, Fox and Friends, The CBS Evening News, The NBC Nightly News, Eye to Eye, CNN's Talk Back Live!, PBS, QVC* and many others. He's a syndicated columnist in 150 newspapers worldwide and his Chicken Soup for the Soul® radio shows are syndicated throughout North America.

As CEO of Chicken Soup for the Soul® Enterprises, a billion-dollar empire that encompasses licensing, merchandising and publishing activities around the globe, Canfield is perhaps the most outwardly accomplished of his peers in *The Secret*. Rhonda Byrne might be on her way to matching that, but most of the other teachers in the film aren't even close.

Rhonda's unflagging drive to produce and distribute her film is an echo of Canfield's in getting his first book with Mark Victor Hansen off the ground. After being rejected by over one hundred publishers and then dropped by their agent, they finally resorted to going booth-by-booth at a publishers' trade show. They eventually landed a no-advance deal with Florida-based Health Communications, Inc. (HCI), now a large and successful independent publisher, but at the time it probably wouldn't have been many authors' first choice, not even Hansen and Canfield's.

Their perseverance is probably what separates them from most authors, indeed most people. Not only did they persist beyond reason in seeking a publisher, they were relentless in promoting their book. When it was first published it didn't immediately catch fire but after an inspirational meeting with a psychic, Canfield tells *Share Guide*'s Dennis Hughes:

> We came up with this idea that we would do five things every single day to promote the book. This could mean signing five books and giving them to people for free. It could be giving talks at churches or sending out free copies to reviewers, or giving five radio interviews. There were five specific actions we did every day so there was always something happening that promoted the book. Eventually, I wrote a letter to the publisher of a publication called *L.A. Parents*. We had a story in the book about

parenting, and I asked them to reprint it. In exchange for printing it, we asked that they put at the bottom a little box that said it was excerpted from *Chicken Soup For The Soul*®. He liked the story so much that he told us there were many more of these parenting magazines all across the country. He helped me to send out this article to every editor and we got 55 copies of it printed. I think that is one of the things that helped the book to take off."[1]

They called it "The Rule of Fives," but it was really good ol' guerilla marketing; working every angle they could to get the word out about the book. This was their secret and they brought that same unrelenting pursuit of success to the whole series of books that ensued after the success of the first, resulting in tens of millions of books being sold around the world.

Canfield, like many of his peers, is very big on coaching. He has business coaches, writing coaches, financial coaches and strategic planning coaches for himself, as well as running a very successful coaching business.

He's also very sophisticated in how he uses the Internet to further awareness of his products, offering free articles for reprint, provided that they are properly credited. I thought it would be worthwhile reprinting one of them here to give a sampling of his motivational writing—but remember, these are ads!

Jack Canfield's Top 7 Success Tips

1) **Take 100% Responsibility for Your Life.** One of the greatest myths that is pervasive in our culture today is that you are entitled to a great life—that somehow, somewhere, someone is responsible for filling our lives with continual happiness, exciting career options, nurturing family time and blissful personal relationships simply because we exist. But the real truth is that there is only one person responsible for the quality of the life you live. That person is YOU.

2) **Be Clear Why You're Here.** I believe each of us is born with a life purpose. Identifying, acknowledging and honoring this purpose is perhaps the most important action successful people take. They take the time to understand what they're here to do—and then they pursue that with passion and enthusiasm.

3) **Decide What You Want.** One of the main reasons why most people don't get what they want is they haven't decided what they want. They haven't defined their desires in clear and compelling detail...What does success look like to you?

4) **Believe It's Possible.** Scientists used to believe that humans responded to information flowing into the brain from the outside world. But today,

they're learning instead that we respond to what the brain, based on previous experience, expects to happen next...In fact, the mind is such a powerful instrument, it can deliver to you literally everything you want. But you have to believe that what you want is possible.

5) **Believe in Yourself.** If you are going to be successful in creating the life of your dreams, you have to believe that you are capable of making it happen... Whether you call it self-esteem, self-confidence or self-assurance, it is a deep-seated belief that you have what it takes—the abilities, inner resources, talents and skills to create your desired results.

6) **Become an Inverse Paranoid.** Imagine how much easier it would be to succeed in life if you were constantly expecting the world to support you and bring you opportunity. Successful people do just that.

7) **Unleash the Power of Goal Setting.** Experts on the science of success know the brain is a goal-seeking organism. Whatever goal you give to your subconscious mind, it will work day and night to achieve...[2]

Lisa Nichols:
The Gift to Inspire and to Empower

Nichols was one of the substitutes for Esther Hicks when Rhonda edited Hicks out of *The Secret*. Likely at the suggestion of Jack Canfield, Byrne recruited Nichols, a successful author of two *Chicken Soup* books (much to the chagrin of Nichols' childhood English teacher, who called her "one of the worst writers.")[3]

What I find refreshing about Nichols is that although she is a true believer in the Law of Attraction, her view of it is not absolutist, as is Rhonda's and those of some of the other teachers in *The Secret*. Nichols concedes that luck exists and that sick children don't necessarily attract cancers to themselves.[4]

In 2000, Nichols founded Motivating the Teen Spirit, LLC, which runs a comprehensive empowerment skills program for teen self-development. According to Nichols' website, "as of January 2007, her company has impacted the lives of over 60,486 teens, prevented over 1,812 suicides, reunited thousands of teens with their parents, and influenced more than 987 teen drop outs to return to school."[5]

Nichols is available as a public speaker, she offers courses and seminars, and one can purchase a variety of her lectures on CD. Companies and organizations small and large have hired Lisa as a speaker all over the world.

A forty-year-old Los Angeles native, she is a single mother and did not achieve success without a good amount of struggle. Raised in LA's notorious South Central, she says, "I grew up in an area that had a lot of crime and violence and bad energy. I didn't consider myself beautiful but I had this dream of becoming an international speaker." Always tight for money, she flunked out of Oregon's Linfield University in the middle of her sophomore year. She followed her dream of becoming a motivational speaker, single-mindedly and with amazing persistence, a common trait in many of *The Secret*'s teachers. She says, "In 1996, I started out by speaking for free for three years, then people started paying me to speak. I didn't get discouraged when I heard the no's. I kept going because I knew that eventually people would find the relevance in what I was doing."[6]

Anyone signing up for Nichols' "Special Report" emails via her website will receive missives beginning much like this one:

> You can dramatically transform your life with this one tip I'm going to give you today. It is so important and so huge that I want you to read this email two or three times every day! Good things will absolutely come your way.
>
> The Law of Attraction begins and ends with gratitude.

I repeat: The Law of Attraction begins and ends with gratitude.

Never, ever forget that. It's perhaps the most critical thing to remember as you apply this wonderful universal law in your life on a day-to-day basis.

Be truly grateful for what you have. The more grateful you are, the more good things will come your way. You will see.

More of the same is to be found in her "Special Report created for viewers of *The Oprah Winfrey Show*" (she was a guest on the Oprah shows that blew up all things *Secret*):

Lisa Nichols' Three Steps to the Law of Attraction, as revealed in the movie *The Secret*:

1) Ask the universe for what you want.

2) Believe that it is already yours.

3) Be ready to receive.

Ask and believe, and you shall receive. Seems almost magical, doesn't it? But, yes, that is how the universe works!

However, Nichols does give more practical advice about

how to make the Law of Attraction work:

> The biggest myth people have about the Law of Attraction is that you simply ask for something, make yourself a cup of tea, sit back, cross your legs, and just wait for the genie to appear, but this is not a passive process.

> There is no part about the Law of Attraction that says be still. You have to be in action about what you want. You've committed to creating something, and the universe gives you the creative ideas and the resources to act and make it happen.

> When you bump into the right person at the right time, it's up to you to follow up and call them back. When the universe sends you an idea for a new book, it's up to you to begin writing.

> You are an active participant in your life, an active participant with the universe. In fact, you will probably become even more active because the Law of Attraction will bring you more opportunities than you ever dreamed.[7]

Marci Shimoff: *Happy for No Reason*

Shimoff describes herself as "the woman's face of the biggest self-help book phenomenon in history, *Chicken*

Soup for the Soul." The author of six books in that series, she has become one of the world's leading female self-help authors.

President and co-founder of the Esteem Group, she delivers keynote addresses and seminars on self-esteem, self-empowerment and peak performance to corporations, professional and non-profit organizations, and women's associations. Her client list contains numerous Fortune 500 companies, including AT&T, General Motors, Sears, Amoco, Western Union, and Bristol-Myers Squibb. She is also a founding member and director of Jack Canfield's Transformational Leadership Council.

An excellent self-promoter, Shimoff is a veteran of more than 500 national and regional television and radio shows; she has been interviewed for over 100 newspaper articles nationwide and her writing has appeared in national women's magazines, including *Ladies Home Journal* and *Woman's World.*

Demonstrating her own high self-esteem, Shimoff is stepping out of the shadow of Jack Canfield and Mark Victor Hansen's *Chicken Soup* series and she is publishing her new book, *Happy for No Reason: Seven Steps to Being Happier Right Now*, under her own steam with Simon & Schuster (notably, publishers of *The Secret*) in December 2007. The promotional copy for the book tells us:

Everyone wants to be happy—it's the goal of all we do.

Yet, so many people are unhappy today: one in five women in America is on anti-depressants! What are we doing wrong? Clearly, we need a new approach to being happy. *Happy for No Reason* presents three startling, new ideas and a practical program that will forever change the way you look at creating happiness in your life:

1. Happiness is not an emotion, a spike of elation or euphoria. True happiness is a lasting, neuro-physio-logical state of peace and well-being.

2. True happiness is not based on what we do or have—it doesn't depend on external reasons or circumstances.

3. Recent research shows that we all have a happiness set-point that is approximately 50% genetic and 50% learned. No matter what happens to us, we tend to return to a set range of happiness. And in the same way that we'd crank up the thermostat to get comfortable on a chilly day, we can actually reprogram our happiness set-point to a higher level of peace and well-being.

We're so busy trying to change our outer world in order to be happier, yet what we really need to do is change our happiness set-point. *Happy for No Reason* shows us how to do just that![8]

Happy For No Reason is also the title of one of her keynote presentations. (The others are: *The Heart of The Secret*; *Chicken Soup for the Soul*; *Chicken Soup for the Woman's Soul*; *and Living with Esteem: Becoming a Peak Performer*). Shimoff, who earned her MBA from UCLA and holds an advanced certificate as a stress management consultant, is clearly feeling happy, but in her case there seems to be ample reason.

5

THE SECRET WEALTH COACHES

"To the person who truly desires to be in tune, total fitness today involves more than a simple body fitness program, it now includes an overall Life Fitness Program. It includes fitness in all areas of daily life. For instance, if your finances are weak and out of shape, and you are under constant worry and frustration over it, how can you expect to have true and total fitness."

Dr. John Demartini
Inspirational Speaker

Although some of these teachers' websites[1] and books might send certain people screaming and running away in the opposite direction, I have had occasion to interact with a couple of them, as well as with several other members of the Transformational Leadership Council. My observation is that, aside from being truly outstanding individuals who are exceptionally loving, intelligent, charming and totally inspiring to be around, they are also marketing geniuses. Personal transformation is their business and the packaging of their programs is designed to appeal to the largest possible audience. Accordingly, while some people from a more jaded or "sophisticated" background might at times find this packaging to be a bit lowbrow, its effectiveness in attracting a broader market cannot be doubted.

Bob Proctor: No Gamble

Author, lecturer, counselor, business consultant, entrepreneur, and self-described "teacher of the gospel of positive thinking," Bob Proctor claims to be in the lineage of Napoleon Hill, Earl Nightingale and Wallace D. Wattles and his mission is to show his clients how to put their teachings into practice and how to achieve success in any endeavor.

Perhaps the reason Bob Proctor is so insightful into the factors that limit peoples' success is rooted in the fact that he lived an aimless, purposeless existence for the first 26 years of his own life. Born in a little town in northern Ontario, Canada with the low self-esteem that often befalls a family's middle child, he performed poorly in school, dropped out and did a hitch in the navy. Afterward he drifted from one dead-end job to another until a friend recognized potential in Bob that he had no awareness of himself. **The friend introduced Bob to the concept of self-development through Napoleon Hill's classic *Think and Grow Rich*.** With the spark generated by Hill's words, Proctor found the initiative to start an office cleaning business which **he grew to international scope in his first year of operation.** From that experience—after seeing what he had been able to accomplish with just a rudimentary knowledge of personal motivation and goal-setting—he hungered for more information. His quest took him to the Nightingale-Conant organization to study under his mentor, Earl Nightingale. Once on board, he rose swiftly through the ranks. Eventually, while the Nightingale-Conant organization assumed the forefront in wide-scale distribution of personal development programs, **Bob felt the need to take his ideas and methods directly to the individual,** to the one-on-one level which had proved so successful for himself (emphases by webmaster).[2]

Proctor is the author of international best-seller *You Were Born Rich* and other works, including *Mission in Commission, The Winner's Image, The Goal Achiever, The Success Series, The Success Puzzle, The Recruiting Puzzle,* and *Being Your Very Best.*

As wowed and impressed as I was by Proctor's segments in *The Secret,* I was equally disappointed by Proctor's latest Internet venture, in partnership with fellow *Secret* teachers Jack Canfield and Michael Beckwith, two other men for whom I have a great deal of respect.

The product they are hawking on the web, "SGR: Science of Getting Rich Seminar," consists of a copy of Wattles' *Science of Getting Rich* book; an MP3 player loaded with the three speakers' motivational lectures; 10 CDs and printed transcripts of the same recordings; "vision boards," (which look exactly like the Quartet® Dry-Erase Boards you can get from Office Depot®; "a Rich, Supple Leather-Bound Briefcase" (which a Chinese slave laborer probably inhaled carcinogenic fumes to sell to the SGR folks for less than a tenth of its actual worth...) and "A Life-Changing Opportunity: Coaching Calls with Bob Proctor."[3] All for just $1,995.

There is doubtless some value in the "SGR" package, but in it I cannot help but detect a rapacious money-grab by these teachers in the wake of *The Secret*'s success. The design of the website from which the program is sold reminds me of Publishers Clearing House circulars from the 1990s and the seminar and digital accoutrements seem a bit overpriced for the target market. We shall see.

Lee Brower: Empowered Wealth

Lee Brower is Founder and CEO of Empowered Wealth, LLC, a consulting firm headquartered in Bountiful,

Utah (one wonders whether they chose the location for its name!). While he doesn't describe himself as such, he's not far from being our favorite teacher occupation, a "wealth coach," advising successful businesses, families, trusts, foundations, professional athletes and celebrities on how to protect and empower their assets. He is also a Managing Partner of Dedicated Radio, LLC and a National Partner for the Private Consulting Group, a boutique broker/dealer that specializes in providing financial solutions and strategies for wealthy families and individuals.

He promotes what he calls The Empowered Wealth System®, The Family Empowered Bank™ concept and The "Relevant" Living Trust™, which he says, "have become cornerstones for the construction of bridges that transport a family's 'True Wealth' to future generations." Hmmm. Well, at least we know he likes a good trademark and service mark when he sees one.

Brower is also partial to a good logo and Empowered Wealth, LLC sports a multicolored quadrant design, representing the four quadrants of "True Wealth," which they describe as:

> **Financial Assets.** Financial Assets are identified with the Southwest Quadrant, which represents what most people think of when they hear the word "assets." In other words, "things"...such as money, investments, businesses, property, etc.

Human Assets. The Northwest Quadrant is your Human Assets. These assets, when fully considered, are of greater worth than your Financial Assets. Included here are the members of your family, health, happiness, heritage, values and many more similar assets.

Intellectual Assets. Intellectual Assets are in the Northeast Quadrant. Most people when they think of Intellectual Assets immediately think of education. Other Intellectual Assets are life's experiences—both good and bad, reputation, strategic alliances, traditions, etc.

Civic Assets. The Southeast Quadrant represents your Civic Assets. The government defines Civic Assets as those assets we must put back into society to do good. They call them taxes. We define Civic Assets as all contributions, of any kind whether Financial, Human, or Intellectual, that employ our assets in the most efficient manner for the benefit of society.[4]

The company considers itself to be the only asset growth and management system that recognizes and focuses on these four asset quadrants. They are probably right.

Loral Langemeier:
This Cowgirl Ain't Got the Blues!

Langemeier was born and raised on a farm in Nebraska. She started her first real business while still attending college classes. In fact, by then, she'd already had the business bug for a while. She tells us:

> [I] started my first business when I was 12, did another one when I was 17, 24, just kept building them. And I'm a major business builder. A lot of people say, "Well, all of this is real estate." Well, I get really wealthy doing real estate, but I really love building businesses and I've been building businesses most of my life in one form or another. I have had mentors as early as I can remember in my teens. I started in the wealth industry. I have a finance degree, so one of my mentors was a local banker who taught me a lot about banking and investing and bank finance, and then decided to go into the health industry, got a Master's Degree in Human Development and Human Behavior, Exercise Physiology, was in the health industry for a long time, and again, just found great mentors that could really help me move through those since I was almost twenty-seven.[5]

She then met Rich Kiyosaki, of *Rich Dad, Poor Dad* fame and famously partner of Donald Trump (how come neither of them are *Secret* teachers, come to think of it?), and for five years, she was the only coach, facilitator, trainer and distributor for the *Rich Dad, Poor Dad* series. They also promoted seventeen or so other motivational speakers and what she terms "wealth builders."

Then, in about 2001, she formed her own company LiveOutLoud, Inc., which is essentially a wealth coaching business, although it is self-described as "a global educational company committed to revolutionizing the way in which people take responsibility for their financial lives. We advocate wealth building for individuals, couples and business partners through the design, development and sale of innovative financial models and tools."[6]

Like several of her *Secret* peers she is a fan of personal branding and she has given herself the sobriquet of "the Millionaire Maker," using it in the title of her books, *The Millionaire Maker: Act, Think and Make Money the Way the Wealthy Do, The Millionaire Maker's Guide to Wealth Cycle Investing* and most recently *The Millionaire Maker's Guide to Creating a Cash Machine for Life*. Depending on what you think of him, this endorsement from ex-hedge fund manager and current TV star Jim Cramer (CNBC's *Mad Money*) may or may not be impressive: "You want to keep up with the Joneses? Be my guest. You want to trounce the Joneses and the rest of the gang? Don't just read this book; act on it."[7]

She believes that Americans have a choice in their financial decisions and that anyone can learn to act, think and make money the way the wealthy do—and have been doing for generations. Loral's programs include her "Wealth Cycle" strategies, which teach people how to generate cash and build wealth through a continuous cycle of assets and income. As part of the Wealth Cycle, she presents how anyone can capitalize on their skills and passions and generate cash—make millions—through building what she calls Cash Machines. A popular and telegenic expert, she's been featured in newspapers and on television programs including *USA Today, Wall Street Journal* and *New York Times* as well as *CNN* and *Fox News*.

In addition to the books, she offers teleseminars, workshops and coaching. Her clients range from individuals and small business owners to large corporations including Chevron, Franklin Covey, Arthur Anderson, Home Depot, Marriott, Dupont and Silicon Graphics.

Langemeier is a big fan of real estate investing, offering something she calls the R.E.A.L. Workshop, standing for Real Estate As Leverage. She tells interviewer Andy O'Bryan:

> What I see is when you really run your real estate like a business, you really are hanging your shield out there saying, "I'm now a real estate investor and I'm building a business for this." It's absolutely doable. We help people quit their jobs and totally become real estate investors. I've transitioned so many people out of their jobs from sales jobs to pilots to airline

attendants to IT consultants to coaches to speakers. I mean, we've helped a lot of people who've quit their jobs become real estate investors full time, but it takes, depending on how much money and how much they already know, anywhere from 6 months to a year to get somebody fully in the business.

Very doable and to me it's one of the greatest wealth builders. You know, I became a millionaire at thirty-four doing it and I mean that in gross assets, we're heading to over fifty million in gross assets, and we've done it literally in about three or four years.[8]

Small wonder that she's a true believer!

John Assaraf: "The Street Kid"

Born in 1961, John Assaraf is co-founder (with Murray Smith) of OneCoach, Inc., a San Diego-based company specializing in training small businesses to succeed. After building seventeen multi-million dollar companies in as many different industries, Assaraf and Smith felt that they had figured out the blueprint for success and they formed their "OneCoach Business Mastery Program."

Assaraf has lived a sort of American dream, perhaps not quite rags to riches, but with a cab driver father, he wasn't exactly groomed for corporate success. He tells us that he was once a street gang member and drug dealer, calling himself "The Street Kid." His breakthrough came at age 21, when he met two businessmen who he describes as "the most successful sub-franchisers of real estate offices in the world [with] 1,500 offices in 19 countries generat[ing] over $15 billion a year in real estate sales."[9] Assaraf partnered with them and was offered the RE/MAX Indiana franchise. He successfully turned that failing office into a massive success. The dotcom boom of the 1990s did not pass him by either, as he led real estate virtual tours company Bamboo.com into a hot IPO in just nine months and, subsequently, a merger with digital imaging company Ipix Corporation.

With his current business OneCoach (the last one was called The Street Kid Company—you can see how attached he is to that nickname), Assaraf and partner Smith have pooled their ideas and have built up another successful business, which they describe as "committed to helping entrepreneurs and professionals grow their small business revenues so they can achieve financial freedom and live extraordinary lives."

Assaraf has appeared on plenty of TV shows, including *Larry King Live, The Ellen DeGeneres Show, ABC, CBS* and *NBC* and he is the author of *The Street Kid's Guide to Having it All*, a bestseller on multiple lists. Like many of the other teachers in *The Secret*, he is also a very well compensated and popular public speaker.

So what does he teach? His mission is to show us how we

can "have it all"—good health, great families, enriching careers, faithful friends, and plenty of spiritual connectedness. He describes the six functions of the conscious mind (reason, will, memory, perception, imagination, and intuition) and the three functions of the subconscious mind (the operator of our bodily functions, the regulator of our habits, and the connector to the rest of the world).

Like many "gurus," Assaraf is prone to making rather oblique pronouncements. In his essay "The One Major Key For Achieving Outstanding Results," he writes:

> Let me explain one simple idea that I know will open your mind to actually understanding your true potential. First and foremost, understand that the intelligence that created you made no errors in her creation. We are pure intelligent energy with amazing capabilities.[10]

David Schirmer: Candy Corn or Con?

If ever there was a teacher open about his materialism, it's Schirmer. His official biography tells us that, "He now drives the car of his dream[s], the latest BMW M5, owns real estate, has numerous businesses and this year will make a personal income from trading and business in excess of $1.5 million."[11]

A self-described wealth coach, entrepreneur and private share investor and trader, Schirmer claims that his "clients have averaged just on 30% per annum over the past 8 years investing in blue chips stocks. The Professional Traders he has taught have returned up to 50% a month consistently. This makes him one of the greatest stock and commodity teachers of our time."[12]

No kidding—to put this into perspective, Warren Buffett, generally regarded as the most successful investor of all time, achieved average annualized returns for the stock investments in his company's (Berkshire Hathaway) portfolio from 1980 to 2003 of 27.09%.[13] This exceeds the average annual return of the most widely followed US stock index, the Standard & Poors 500, by 12.24% over this time period. One wonders why we haven't heard more about Mr. Schirmer, given his Buffett-busting success. Can we attribute it to Melbourne, Australia being further from the media spotlight than Omaha, Nebraska?[14]

Well, the awful truth may be that Schirmer is a con artist and thief. Soon after Schirmer made this well-chuffed post on *The Secret* Forum:

Posted by David Schirmer 05/24/07 07:18 AM

Re: What made you smile today?
When a well meaning, high profile psychologist on a radio interview said today that the Secert [sic] is dangerous and doesn't work...and what professional

qualifactions [sic] do I have to back up my claims! I calmly replied that I have a degree in results...and the "By your fruits you are known!" I had to smile as I looked out from my window of my office at home across the estate to the city, as he was stuck in traffic driving his basic car home from the job he goes to every day!!!![15]

The Australian tabloid news show, *A Current Affair* aired the first of several interview segments with Schirmer's investors, students and former employees, all alleging that he had bilked them out of a combined total of several hundreds of thousands of dollars. In an ambush set-up, where Schirmer thought he was being interviewed about his investing genius on the show's soundstage, with cameras rolling on a close-up of Schirmer's face, the host confronted him with clips of the victims' interviews. In my opinion, Schirmer reacted like a classic sociopath.[16] For whatever it's worth, Schirmer posted a rebuttal on YouTube.[17]

6

MIND TECHNOLOGY

"Brain Wave Patterns 101: The first thing you need to know is that 24 hours a day, nerve cells in your brain are generating electrical impulses that fluctuate rhythmically in distinct patterns called brain wave patterns— patterns closely correlated with your thoughts, your emotions, your state of being, the functioning of the various systems of your body, and, in essence the entire quality of your life!"

www.Centerpointe.com

Some of the most interesting speakers in *The Secret* have devoted their lives to studying the mechanisms of human cognition and the psyche. Their aim is to improve performance in any number of endeavors and in the general quality of life, through a better understanding of the human mind.

Bill Harris & Holosync®

In June 2007, I had occasion to work as a Second Unit Director on the shoot for a documentary with the working title, *The Gift*, featuring several members of the Transformational Leadership Council, including *The Secret*'s Bill Harris. This took place on the incredible SeaDream megayacht, chartered by Make a Change Personal Discovery Journeys® organized by Sydney Cresci, on a cruise of the French and Italian Rivieras.

During the day, the film crew and speakers would go ashore to shoot interviews in beautiful Mediterranean villages and then return to the yacht in the evenings to shoot their lectures. The extreme luxury of this yacht, which has been awarded the highest ratings by *Condé Nast Traveler, Travel & Leisure*, and *Berlitz*, and the stunning beauty of the ports we visited were outshone only by the remarkable personalities of the speakers.

I would highly recommend taking a Make a Change Personal Discovery Journeys® cruise to whomever can afford it.[1] Luckily for me, I got to ride for free (granted, I was working 16-hour days, shooting a film).

The opportunity to socialize with Bill Harris and his delightful fiancée, Denise, along with many of the other exceptional speakers there, gave me a great insight into the business of personal and corporate transformation as I listened to them talk shop.

I also formed a deep admiration and appreciation for these loving people, who treated me better than practically anyone ever had done in my life. It was indescribably wonderful. These folks are an outstanding, fascinating community of people who have made successful careers by creating programs to help other people.

Bill Harris has a delightfully sharp-witted, curmudgeonly sense of humor, which I found to be totally unexpected. I figured that someone who had designed one of the most successful meditation programs in the world would be a mellow dude, so his acerbic feistiness was not lost on me one bit; as a New Yorker, I appreciate that stuff!

Bill Harris is the President and Director of Centerpointe Research Institute and he has a rich and fascinating biography, including three years of graduate study in music, studying with world-renowned Czech composer Tomas Svoboda and Spanish composer Salvador Brotons, and playing saxophone, flute, clarinet, and piano professionally for over 40 years. He's also a private pilot and CEO of Mercury Aviation, LLC.

The greatest impact he has had on the world at-large has been through Centerpointe. Founded by Harris and former partner Wes Wait in 1989, over 300,000 people in 173 countries have participated in the Institute's programs.

The best known of its products is the Holosync® audio

meditation program. As described by Centerpointe, inventors Harris and Wait used electronic tone generators and frequency counters borrowed from a local university to record master soundtracks for a series of 13 program levels:

> The initial idea was to re-create, with modern high-tech methods, the meditation experience usually reserved to those dedicated few willing to meditate many hours each day for many years. To recreate the second ingredient of the meditation process—the "rescripting" that takes place as meditators reach an altered, meditative state and then reprogram their unconscious mind through mantras, affirmations, or prayers—they added, beginning with the second level of the program, silent affirmations chosen by the participant and recorded in his or her own voice, and delivered using Centerpointe's proprietary Autofonix® silent messaging technology.[2]

It utilizes binaural beats to help a person achieve different meditative states that further one's capacity to handle stress, and to feel more at peace. At least, that's the claim and Harris isn't bashful about boiling it down to a high-concept sales pitch, writing in email, "with The Holosync® Solution, you'll meditate deeper than a Zen Monk at the push of a button. And, as recent research proves, you'll not only live happier with daily meditation, but you'll live longer too." For more of the official line on how it works, visit the Centerpointe website and access the article "Special Report: How The Holosync®️ Technology Works."[3]

In a conversation between Bill Harris and Ken Wilber published in the latter's *Integral Naked* magazine, they discussed how research shows that there are at least two concepts necessary for an adequate understanding of consciousness: states and stages. Everyone, including infants, experiences the three main natural states of consciousness: 1) waking, 2) dreaming and 3) sleeping. Although some people occasionally experience lucid dreaming, most people are consciously aware only during wakefulness.

Through practices such as meditation, one can develop stages that allow one to transform the temporary states (such as the longer brainwave states associated with hyperconsciousness) into *permanent abilities* that can be accessed at will. Ken explains that stages of consciousness unfold and develop over time, creating structures in the psyche (or actually in the neural pathways, according to other researchers[4]), allowing higher states of awareness to become permanent acquisitions. Ken supports the idea that brain-mind machines can induce changes in brain states and accelerate growth through the stages of consciousness, and he recently endorsed the Holosync®️ to the subscribers of his email newsletter.

Using Holosync®️ equipment, if a frequency of 100 Hz is played into one ear and a frequency of 108 Hz is played into the other, the brain will naturally synchronize at the difference between the two: 8 Hz. This is the "binaural beat," and in this example, the brain would shift into a low-alpha state. Brain-wave technologies have been demonstrated to help shift participants into alpha, theta, and even delta brain states. Moreover, as the carrier frequencies are changed, various types of deepening of brain states have been observed.

This suggests that as Holosync® can help one induce brain states (such as theta-alpha) that normally would take many months to achieve using meditation alone. Repeated exposure to altered consciousness states helps one develop through consciousness stages, which cannot be skipped, but must be repeated via induction of brain states. Correlative consciousness states appear to accelerate growth through the various stages. So, although the use of brain-mind technologies is not necessary for growth, development, or meditative enlightenment, it appears that they can help accelerate the process.

The most acute question that you can ask of a technology like this is "Does it really work?" In reading a review of Holosync®, I was reminded of the comment of a friend using another set of meditation CDs, Robert Monroe's Hemi-Sync®,[5] who said she couldn't stay awake long enough to find out whether or not they worked. (Incidentally, Harris credits Monroe with helping him to develop the technology on which Holosync® is based.)

Writing at Buzzle.com, Gigi Konwin says, "Unlike the other testimonials you may have read, I did not experience profound changes after listening to the first CD. In fact, for the most part, I fell asleep! But that's okay, because the more I listened, the less sleeping I did. Truth be told, I still doze off when I'm starting a new level. Each new level takes you into deeper meditative states and requires an adjustment." At the time of writing, she'd been using the program for two years, an hour a day nearly every day. And while not being unreservedly enthusiastic, she seems to think it works for her:

> I'm calmer
> I rarely get angry.
> I have a more positive attitude.
> I've become more spiritual.
> I'm happier—negative thoughts creep in, but they don't stay.[6]

There are certainly plenty of users of the CDs and many of them believe they have achieved worthwhile results. There are also quite a few dissatisfied customers as evidenced by a quick bit of surfing on the web, but you can't please 'em all.

Anyone who visits the official *The Secret* website is invited to join various members' groups, sign up for newsletters and so forth. One of the most active of these is called "The Masters of *The Secret* with Bill Harris."[7] Each week after signing up (for free) you receive an email from

Harris inviting you to log on to hear a conversation with other teachers from *The Secret*, such as James Ray, Lisa Nichols, John Assaraf, Hale Dwoskin, Michael Beckwith and Jack Canfield.

Hale Dwoskin & The Sedona Method

Dwoskin is the author of the *The Sedona Method: Your Key to Lasting Happiness, Success, Peace and Emotional Well-being* and CEO and Director of Training of Sedona Training Associates. He co-founded the company in 1996 to teach courses based on the emotional releasing techniques originated by his mentor, Lester Levenson. He describes his meeting with Levenson:

> In 1976, I met Lester Levenson, the man who inspired the creation of the Sedona Method who would also become my mentor. Back then, I was an ardent, although confused, seeker who had gone to numerous seminars led by teachers from both the East and the West. I had studied various body-centered disciplines, including yoga, tai chi, and shiatsu. I had actively participated in numerous personal growth courses, including EST, Actualism, Theta Seminars, and Rebirthing. At these seminars, I had many nice experiences and heard and under-stood—at least intellectually—many useful concepts. Still, I felt incomplete. I longed for a simple and powerful answer to some important yet vexing

questions like: "What is my life's purpose?" "What is truth?" "Who am I?" and "How can I feel at home and at peace with my life?" Much of what I heard and experienced only added to my questioning. No one seemed to have truly satisfying answers or to have truly satisfied themselves about their true nature. There was also a strong, almost universal belief that growing was hard work that required baring your soul and reliving painful, unresolved issues. That all changed during my very fortunate encounter with this remarkable man.[8]

He goes on to relate how in Levenson's "releasing" technique he finally found what he'd been looking for. In 1987 he moved to Phoenix, Arizona, to work with Levenson for the remainder of the latter's life. At Levenson's request he then moved to Sedona two years later, where Dwoskin met his wife, Amy. By the early '90s, his relationship with Levenson blossomed to the point where the latter turned over the copyrights of his teachings, asking him to continue his work.

I maintained the organization that he'd established towards this end until two years after his death. Then, in 1996, I decided it would be much more effective for Amy and me to start a new company, Sedona Training Associates, to convey the Method to the world in an even bigger way.[9]

The Sedona Method had been created by Levenson after he fell seriously ill in 1952 and doctors told him that he had just weeks to live. According to the Sedona website,

> Lester turned to the laboratory within, seeking a way to revoke his pending death sentence. What he discovered in his exploration was that by releasing his non-love feelings, his health began to improve. Continuing with this experiment, he found that over a 3-month period, he had attained not only renewed health but actually perfect health and perfect peace of mind which lasted 42 years beyond his doctors' expectations.[10]

In a nutshell, the company aims to transform the lives of others in just as dramatic a fashion, and thousands of individuals, as well hundreds of key executives from companies such as Exxon, AT&T, Merrill Lynch, J.C. Penney, Marriott Hotels, FAA, Bristol-Myers, Chemical Bank, Chase Manhattan Bank, Polaroid, Bull, Lever Brothers, Monsanto, Touche Ross, and Mutual of New York have taken the Sedona Method course.

Dwoskin's company cites a study by Dr. Richard J. Davidson of the State University of New York in collaboration with Dr. David C. McClelland of Harvard University as an emphatic endorsement of the effectiveness of the Sedona Method, emblazoning the logo of Harvard Medical School prominently around the website and promotional materials. I was not able to find the original study, but according to Sedona Training Associates the doctors concluded that:

> The Sedona Method is an outstanding technique for its simplicity, efficiency, absence of questionable concepts and rapidity of observable results including significant reduction in heart rate and diastolic blood pressure.[11]

Perhaps the promotional materials are a bit over-the-top, but thousands have taken the course and there are numerous testimonials from participants, as well as endorsements from others in the self-help field, including this one from Jack "Chicken Soup" Canfield:

> Through my work with *Chicken Soup for the Soul* and through my Self-Esteem Seminars, I have been exposed to many self-improvement techniques and processes. This one stands head and shoulders above the rest for the ease of its use, its profound impact, and the speed with which it produces results. The Sedona Method is a vastly accelerated way of letting go of feelings like anger, frustration, jealousy, anxiety, stress, and fear, as well as many other problems even physical pain with which almost everybody struggles at one time or another.[12]

Denis Waitley:
NASA's Explorer of Human Potential

You have to hand it to Denis Waitley, he's gotten some great press:

"Denis Waitley's motivation is more than money. His mission is to tell people they have more control over their destiny than they believe."

—*USA Today*

"Waitley has a quieter, softer style than other merchants of inspiration. He preaches the importance of basic virtues in business—integrity, self-esteem and responsibility."

—*Fortune*

"Vince Lombardi power in a Bob Newhart personality!"

—*Washington Post*

"Soft-spoken and low-key, but what he has to say is mentally exciting. Waitley has counseled Apollo astronauts, Superbowl athletes and Fortune 500 executives, as well as helped U.S. Olympic champions enhance their performance."

—*U.S. News & World Report*

"Denis Waitley is the man who aims folks in the direction of success. He stares you straight in the eye when you meet and while you speak. The two years he spoke to an

NFL football team, they lost only one game and won the Super Bowl twice."

—*Philadelphia Enquirer*

"Interestingly, an American author, Denis Waitley has the best-selling business book in the Mandarin Chinese language during the past decade."

—*Asian Wall Street Journal*

What on earth can he have done to deserve that kind of praise? A graduate of the US Naval Academy at Annapolis and former Navy pilot, he holds a Ph.D. in Human Behavioral Psychology and is a sort of super-counselor. As noted by *U.S. News & World Report*, his clients have included countless corporations bearing household names, including AT&T, Pacific Bell, IBM, Kodak, Sony, Federal Express, Bank of America, Phillip Morris, Merrill Lynch, Microsoft, Ford, General Motors, Chrysler and Standard Oil. As president of the International Society for Advanced Education, inspired by Dr. Jonas Salk, he counseled returning POWs from Vietnam and conducted simulation and stress management seminars for Apollo astronauts.

He says he receives ten speaking requests a day, has sold over ten million audio programs in fourteen languages, and is the author of fifteen non-fiction books, including several international best sellers, *Seeds of Greatness*, *Being the Best*, *The Winner's Edge*, *The Joy of Working*, and *Empires of the Mind*. Needless to say, you can buy his books and audio courses at his website. He also offers an audio book version of the Wallace D. Wattles classic, *The Science of Getting Rich*, of which he says:

> When I first met Rhonda Byrne, creator of *The Secret*, we shared the fact that *The Science of Getting Rich*, written in 1910, nearly a century ago, is a cornerstone in our own belief systems. I attribute much of my own success to my internalization of The Law of Attraction, Thinking and Acting in a Certain Way, The Impression of Increase, and Gratitude, which are core values both in Wallace D. Wattles' book, and in the global phenomenon, *The Secret*.[13]

Waitley offers a handful of short articles for reprint on his website. To get a sense of his wisdom, I've included one below. If it doesn't exactly seem like mind-blowing stuff, remember that a great deal of the impact made by these teachers comes from their verbal delivery. Many of them, including Waitley, have streaming audio and/or video of themselves on their websites, so you might want to visit their sites (see FURTHER READING section, pages 189–191) and then imagine them delivering the various quotes included in this book.

Three Rules for Turning Stress Into Success
by Denis Waitley

1. **Accept the Unchangeable**—Everything that has happened in your life to this minute is unchangeable. It is history. The greatest waste of energy is in looking back at missed opportunities, lamenting past events, grudge collecting, getting even, harboring ill will, and any vengeful thinking. Success is the only acceptable form of revenge. By forgiving your trespassers, you become free to concentrate on going forward with your life and succeeding in spite of your detractors. You will live a rewarding and fulfilling life.

   Your enemies, on the other hand, will forever wonder how you went on to become so successful without them and in the shadow of their doubts.

   Action Idea: Write down on a sheet of paper things that happened in the past that bother you. Now crumple the paper into a ball and throw it at the person teaching this program at the front of the room. This symbolizes letting go of past misfortunes.

2. **Change the Changeable**—What you can change is your reaction to what others say and do. And you can control your own thoughts and actions by dwelling on desired results instead of the penalties of failure. The only real control you have in life is that of your immediate thought and action. Since most of what

we do is a reflex, subconscious habit, it is wise not to act on emotional impulse. In personal relations, it is better to wait a moment until reason has the opportunity to compete with your emotions.

Action Idea: Write down in your diary one thing you will do tomorrow to help you relax more during and after a stressful day.

3. **Avoid the Unacceptable**—Go out of your way to get out of the way of potentially dangerous behaviors and environments. When people tailgate you on the freeway, change lanes. If they follow you at night, drive to a well-lighted public place.

When there are loud, obnoxious people next to you at a restaurant or club, change tables, or locations. Also, be cautious of personal relationships developed via the Internet. With the massive number of individuals surfing the net, the number of predators increases in like proportion. Always be on the alert for potentially dangerous situations involving your health, personal safety, financial speculation and emotional relationships.

Action Idea: What is one unacceptable behavior you have or allow others to do to you that you will avoid starting tomorrow? Example: The way you drive, being around negative people, walking down dark streets alone late at night, etc.[14]

7

THE SECRET SCIENCE

> "Those who use physics to 'prove'
> what they want to believe spiritually
> are on the wrong track and look very
> foolish to real scientists."

Bill Harris

Inventor, Musician, Teacher, Entrepeneur

There are vague allusions to the quantum mechanical underpinnings of *The Secret* in both the film and the book. However, the chapter that most directly engages science does not advertise it very strongly with its title, "The Secret to You," where Rhonda admits that she has never had a great interest in this area.

I never studied science or physics at school, and yet when I read complex books on quantum physics I understood them perfectly because I wanted to understand them. The study of quantum physics helped me to have a deeper understanding of *The Secret*, on an energetic level. For many people, their belief is strengthened when they see a perfect correlation between the knowledge of *The Secret* and the theories of new science.[1]

The Secret associates quantum physics with the Law of Attraction but not as strongly as the 2005 breakout inspirational film, *What The Bleep Do We Know!?* did, in invoking quantum physics as the basis of its "You Create Your Own Reality" credo. Viewers of the latter film will recognize the faces of Fred Alan Wolf and John Hagelin, both of whom have superpowers of quantum tunneling onto the set of any low budget film in need of physicists willing to speak about the relationship between human consciousness and subatomic events, *pro bono*.

Fred Alan Wolf, "Dr. Quantum"

Although much of his interview in *The Secret* ended up on the cutting room floor, Wolf is the best prepared of all the speakers in the film to offer any scientific corroboration of its claims.

I've previously referred to this successful author as "the quantum physics popstar." Wolf has been writing popular books on the subject since the mid-'80s, using his incredible knack for making the most abstract physics hypotheses accessible to the amateur, while melding these concepts with the transpersonal teachings of Eastern mysticism.

In Wolf's latest book, *The Yoga of Time Travel: How the Mind Can Defeat Time*, he describes how many concepts found in ancient and Eastern spiritual traditions are compatible with contemporary physical theory, pointing to the old legends saying that time is the progenitor of the cosmos and that time itself is the child of consciousness.

> Digging deeper into the ancient texts, we find that they say time and space are products of the mind and do not exist independent of it. The principles of quantum physics, remarkably, tell us the same thing. This is an extraordinary key. The trick to going outside the confines of space and time is to reach beyond their source—the mind itself. Paradoxically, we need a theoretical picture created by the mind to understand what it means to reach beyond the mind...
>
> In the early part of the first millennium BCE, Indian philosophers found evidence for the beginnings of what we today call the perennial philosophy. It can be stated in three sentences:

1. An infinite, unchanging reality exists hidden behind the illusion of ceaseless change.

2. This infinite, unchanging reality lies at the core of every being and is the substratum of the personality.

3. Life has one main purpose: to experience this one reality—to discover God while living on earth.[2]

In the same book, Wolf claims that more and more physicists are beginning to extrapolate their subatomic observations to the familiar, macroscopic scale, suggesting that the action of our observing the environment causes the surrounding superposition of probabilities to "solidify" into what we perceive as reality. Wolf says that the application of quantum equations to macro-reality has become a de facto procedure:

> Until very recent times, it was believed that quantum physics only applied to the atomic and subatomic world, a world that was well below human perception. Today, scientists believe that quantum physical effects can also be observed on a larger time and space scale, well within the world of human perception...much as statistical laws are the basis for constructing actuarial tables, quantum physics laws let us calculate very accurately the probabilities for events to occur, even while they remain completely in the dark about the actual events themselves.[3]

However, conservative and liberal scientists alike despise the way unscrupulous businesses seek to legitimize their products by invoking the highfalutin' science of quantum physics in the marketing of New Age-style products.

Yogic, Quantum Magick

Wolf suggests that quantum physics points to something preceding space, time and matter. Wolf calls it sub-spacetime; others, such as deceased Harvard psychiatrist John Mack, have called it the "imaginal realm"; physicist Amit Goswami calls it a "transcendent, nonmaterial, archetypal domain of *potentia*"; anesthesiologist/ physicist Stuart Hameroff calls it a "universal proto-conscious mind which we access, and can influence us...[it] exists at the fundamental level of the universe, at the Planck scale"; and physicist emeritus Roger Penrose has described it as an "idealistic" reality, akin to Plato's world of ideas. In present-day quantum theory, it is conceived as "infinitely dimensional space"...the Australian Aborigines might call this space "Dreamtime."

In his book, *The Yoga of Time Travel*, Wolf posits that consciousness plays a role on the most fundamental level of matter and that yoga and meditation can help people develop their ability to focus and to unfocus—and thus affect the "squaring" and "unsquaring" of *possibility*-waves, opening the door to new possibilities in the world of manifestation.

As an exercise to heal one's past, one could train one's awareness on a focal point where *possibility*-waves from the past meet and merge with *possibility*-waves from the present moment, thus squaring and producing a new probability-curve; this could be seen as a kind of parallel universe "therapy." Likewise, awareness could be trained on a focal point where *possibility*-waves from the future meet and merge with *possibility*-waves from the present, magnetizing an event to one's present, as a kind of parallel universe magick.

> I know it is nearly unthinkable, and perhaps seems even ridiculous to entertain such notions but the past is not fixed in spite of our present memories. Each time a switch takes place reconnecting to a new past parallel universe with the present universe, history changes as we remember it, and we emerge in the new parallel universe with memories now consistent with it.

> However, for big changes to be made in the past involving parallel universes, my research suggests that many people would be needed. It works like a hologram: the more area of the hologram being illumined, the stronger the "signal" and the greater and more real becomes the image. Smaller changes—individual changes—can be accomplished individually or in a small group.[4]

Wolf describes human consciousness as sequences of triplets: defocusing, focusing and defocusing, which is why perception of reality tends to blur and spread out after a focused moment. Wolf posits that through focusing and defocusing, time is created, making time travel intrinsic to the way that mind functions and the way time works. In

Wolf's view, time and mind can have the same meaning.

> ...the importance of consciousness as an element in physics is becoming apparent, and the link between time and consciousness has been forged. The seat of consciousness—the soul or essential self—now appears to be directly involved with time, possibly with its very emergence as something we think we can objectify... Consciousness acts or has an effect on physical matter by making choices that then become manifest. It now appears that such an action cannot simply take place mechanically. Implied now is a "chooser," or subject who affects the brain and nervous system. Some physicists, such as [Henry] Stapp, believe that this chooser arises in the brain through past conditioning. [Roger] Penrose believes the action of choosing takes place nonalgorithmically—that is, not through the action of any mathematical formula or any computer-like process. I suggest that this chooser/observer does not exist in spacetime and is not material, which suggests that it is a spiritual essence or being residing outside of spacetime.[5]

John Hagelin: President of the United States Peace Government

Even though he doesn't get very much screen time, John Hagelin is one of the most interesting characters appearing in *The Secret*. This three-time US Presidential candidate ran on the ticket of Maharishi Mahesh Yogi's now-defunct Natural Law Party, under the slogan "Bringing the light of science into politics" in 1992, 1996 and again in 2000, after failing to beat Pat Buchanan for the nomination to run for the Reform Party.

Prior to his association with TM™, Hagelin received his Physics Ph.D. from Harvard and later did research at Europe's CERN and Stanford University's SLAC facilities. Papers to which he contributed on unified field and superstring theories have been among the most often cited in the field of theoretical physics.

> Dr. Hagelin is currently Director of the Institute of Science, Technology and Public Policy, a leading science and technology think tank, and International Director of the Global Union of Scientists for Peace, an organization of leading scientists throughout the world dedicated to ending nuclear proliferation and establishing lasting world peace. Dr. Hagelin also serves as President of the United States Peace Government, a knowledge-based, complementary government composed of hundreds of America's top scientists, which advocates proven, prevention-oriented solutions to critical social problems; and Minister of Science and Technology of the Global Country of World Peace, an international organization dedicated to prevention-oriented government, world peace, and global administration through natural law.[6]

If you are wondering why you have never heard of these groups, it's because they are organs of the Maharishi Mahesh Yogi's Transcendental Meditation™ movement, founded in 1958 and perhaps the grand-daddy of all "New Age"-type businesses and definitely one of the most successful, claiming to have a current worldwide membership of 3 million[7] and an initiation fee of "only" $2,500.

The movement's "Natural Law" is based on the Maharishi's melding of ancient Hindu cosmology with modern physical theory, which the yogi studied as a youth for a couple of years at Allahabad University in Northern India before dropping out.

Hagelin's 1998 book, *Manual for a Perfect Government*, links quantum physics with consciousness and claims to hold the key to eliminating the problems of crime, terrorism, poor health care, drug abuse, poverty and the weak educational system. Moreover, the book illustrates Hagelin's complete alignment with Maharishi's Transcendental Meditation™ teachings.

I have written elsewhere about the troubling claims of former TM™ members, that the Maharishi is a megalomaniac bent on establishing a Hindu theocracy worldwide based on 4,500-year old Vedic laws, that call for the instatement of a caste system.

Somehow, I think the world will be safe from this plight.

Both as a candidate of the Natural Law Party and as a would-be defense contractor, Hagelin has advocated the "Vedic Defense Shield" as a remedy for most of our national and international problems.

> During the Kosovo air strikes, for example, Hagelin held a press conference to suggest the deployment of 7,000 professional Transcendental Meditation counselors into the Kosovo region to "quickly calm the tensions [and] end the bloodshed"—for a cost of "just" $33 million in tax dollars.[8]

TM™ has had much better luck hustling the US government via the National Institutes of Health (NIH), which has spent more than $21 million funding research on the effects of the Transcendental Meditation technique on heart disease.[9] In 1999, the NIH awarded a grant of nearly $8 million to Maharishi University of Management to establish the first research center specializing in natural preventive medicine for minorities in the US.

In order to qualify for government subsidies, such as the inclusion of TM™ in public school curricula, the Maharishi group has strongly refused to be classified as a religion, calling itself a "mental technique for deep rest." In 1979, the United States Third Circuit Court of Appeals affirmed the lower court decision in *Malnak v. Yogi* that TM™ could not be taught in New Jersey public schools because it violated the separation of church and state. The mantras used are apparently invocations to Hindu deities. Nevertheless, TM™ continues to be taught at a few charter public schools in other states.

One man's "technique" is another man's "religion," is another man's "cult" and a 1995 Parliamentary Commission on Cults in France named Transcendental Meditation™, Jehovah's Witnesses, Christian Scientists, Rosicrucians, the Church of Scientology and Baptists as cults/sects.

As I've said elsewhere, I doubt that Transcendental Meditation™ is any more nefarious to global interests than Lockheed Martin. If the TMers are able to successfully hustle a piece of the US Defense Budget with their meditation program, I say more power to 'em...

John Demartini &
The Breakthrough Experience®

John Demartini has been described to me by a friend who has met him on three occasions and who has taken his Breakthrough Experience® seminar as one the most astoundingly intelligent, dynamic, well-read and mind-blowing individuals whom he has ever encountered in his life, saying Demartini's ability to speedily access the vast library of information that he has read is simply incredible. In private, Demartini credits his abilities with a near death experience he had while he was a panhandling high school dropout living in a lean-to on the beach as a surfer dude in Hawaii. He contracted severe strychnine poisoning and hovered on the edge of death for several days and emerged from this experience with greatly enhanced cognition. On his website, he says:

> After being given a second chance I made the decision to dedicate my life to becoming a teacher, healer and philosopher. I have been working on that mission for thirty years now. I became a doctor of chiropractic and clinical research to understand the essence of healing. I became a professional speaker to master the art of teaching and I became a student of science, theology and philosophy to understand our connection with the divine.[10]

I noted to my friend that Demartini seems to use the term "quantum physics" quite frequently in reference to his methods and my friend assured me that if anyone in the self-help circuit understands the theories of quantum physics, Demartini most certainly does.

The Breakthrough Experience®, which my friend took and raved about is an intense two-day seminar, which exercises The Demartini Method®:

> Derived from a study of Quantum Physics, The Demartini Method® is [a] predetermined set of questions and actions that neutralizes your emotional charges and brings balance to your mind and body. A fully reproducible science you can take home with

you, it enables you to discover the underlying order governing your apparent daily chaos.

This unique program helps you experience a marked increase in your productivity and provides you with a new language for achieving significant and lasting change. Its benefits and results are tailored to your specific issues and concerns. You walk away knowing that this was truly one of the most valued and rewarding events of your life.[11]

Apparently, The Breakthrough Experience® is all that it's cracked up to be. One thing my friend mentioned about Demartini's teachings that I thought was very interesting is that he says that human beings relate to each other based on their predetermined empirical value systems which they hold to be true. The result is that *people do not actually relate to each other, they relate to their own value systems!* My friend said that the exercises which illuminated this were absolutely profound and stunning.

A die-hard proponent of unconditional love, Demartini is the founder of the Concourse of Wisdom School of Philosophy, which has different branches that address 1) Personal & Professional Development; 2) Corporate Development; and 3) Chiropractic & Health Professional Development.

Demartini's "Total Life Fitness Questionnaire is reproduced here to give you an idea if his focus:

Total Life Fitness Questionnaire

Physical Fitness:

Do you walk at least one mile or its equivalent once a day?

Are you within 10 pounds of your normal and healthy weight?

Do you work out enough to work up a sweat at least twice a week?

Do you have consistent moderation in the quantity of your eating?

Do you have a consistent rhythm in the timing of your eating?

Do you receive adequate hours of sleep each day (six to eight hours)?

Do you like your body and are you proud of it?

Do you stretch out each of your joints at least twice weekly?

Mental Fitness:

Do you look forward to getting up and making the most of your day?

Are you excited about new ideas and look forward to learning?

Do you read something inspiring and uplifting and about what you love daily?

Do you hang out with idea generating people with mind stimulating ideas?

If you are down or depressed do you, instead of wallowing in it, make an effort to change your action state and do something productive?

If you are scattered and overwhelmed do you stop to prioritize your actions?

Do you have a mentor that helps you not reinvent wheels?

Do you take a moment to visualize and affirm your desired outcomes daily?

Spiritual Fitness:

Do you take a moment for meditative silence daily?

Do you stop and count your blessings at least five minutes daily?

Do you center yourself and listen to your heart before speaking?

Do you open up and share your love with others?

Do you write thank you letters?

Do you visit parks, museums, art galleries or places of worship regularly?

Do you believe their is a higher purpose for each of the events in your life?

Do you treat others the way you want to be treated?

Career Fitness:

Do you love what you do and do what you love?

Do you have clearly set and written career goals?

Do you have an organized work environment?

Do you break large projects into smaller more manageable pieces and work from priorities?

Do you practice and polish your skills regularly?

Can and do you seek advice when needed?

Do you reward yourself for you accomplishments?

Can you accept valid and constructive criticism?

Family Fitness:

Do you have someone special you romantically love?

Do you let your loved ones know how much they mean to you?

Do you take time for family gatherings?

Do you make an effort to do those extra specials with those you love regularly?

Do you really listen when your loved ones speak?

Can you truly be yourself around your family members?

Do you let other family members receive the limelight without jealousy?

Are you proud to be in the family you're in?

Social Fitness:

Are you willing to take on leadership?

Can you join into a group as a team player easily?

Are you outgoing and friendly with a sense of humor?

Are you able to listen attentively and follow instructions?

Do you get out and meet new people, at least one new person a week?

Do you make it a point to help others reach their dreams?

Are you supportive of other people's accomplishments?

Do you speak up and influence others with your ideas?

Financial Fitness:

Do you feel worthy enough to allow yourself to receive money and wealth?

Do you pay yourself and taxes first, not last?

Do you have a regular savings program?

Do you prioritize your spending?

Do you abstain from the overuse of credit cards?

Do you pre-plan your shopping and not impulse buy?

Do you avoid wiping out your savings just because of minor emergencies?

Do you have a separate savings program for vacations?[12]

Give yourself 5 points for every question to which you answered "yes" and zero for those to which you answered "no." According to Demartini, if your score is between 215 and 280, your total life fitness is excellent. If your score is between 145 and 210, your total life fitness is good but this scoring area is an easy place in which to become complacent and you can work towards excellence by taking the steps necessary to be able to answer "yes" to more of the questions to which you answered "no." (I scored 195, so I better get crackin'!) If your score is below 140, you've got some work to do. The implication of course, is that "Total Life Fitness" would be reflected by a "yes" answer to every one of the above questions.

Demartini is the prolific author of six books, including: *How to Make One Hell of a Profit and Still Get to Heaven*, *Count Your Blessings: The Healing Power of Gratitude and Love*, *You Can Have an Amazing Life in Just 60 Days!*, *The Breakthrough Experience*, *The Heart of Love: How to Go Beyond Fantasy to Find True Relationship Fulfillment*.

An interesting factoid about Demartini is that although he has homes all over the world, his main residence is aboard a luxury cruise liner, "The World," "the only resort community to continually circumnavigate the globe."[13]

Does Quantum Physics Support the Law of Attraction?

What does mainstream quantum physics have to say about the Law of Attraction and where do some of the physicists interviewed in *The Secret* stand on this? More importantly, do we really attract our own reality?

Newsweek reported that both John Hagelin and Fred Alan Wolf, the two physicists who appear in the film, "...distanced themselves from the idea of a physical law that attracts necklaces to people who wish for them. 'I don't think it works that way,' says Wolf dryly. 'It hasn't worked that way in my life.' Hagelin acknowledges the larger point, that 'the coherence and effectiveness of our thinking is crucial to our success in life.' But, he adds, 'this is not, principally, the result of magic.'"[14]

"Quantum physics" is a term that gets knocked around quite a bit in the self-help industry. Despite its practical applications in thousands of everyday products, from computers to cell phones, the main thing one needs to know about quantum physics it is that it is largely theoretical and that there are as many interpretations of the foundational theories as there are people willing to bandy the term about. As Fred Alan Wolf says on his website:

> So far there are many, perhaps four main, interpretations of quantum physics currently in use. They are the Bohr collapse postulate, the Cramer transactional postulate, the Everett parallel worlds postulate, and the Bohm hidden variable postulate. They all differ in what they say the world is made of, but they all are based on the quantum physics mathematical laws describing a quantum wavefunction.[15]

Quantum physics deals with infinite possibilities overlapping in what is called a *superposition*. Fred Alan Wolf coined the term "possibility-wave" to describe a sub-unit of a superposition of possibilities. The conventional view, put forth by Niels Bohr (1885–1962) is that a "possibility-wave" squares itself, producing a probability curve when an observation occurs—but as of yet, no one has fully explained how this happens.

To answer this question, physicist John G. Cramer's "Transactional Postulate" calculates the probability of an event, by multiplying a possibility-wave by the time-reversed mirror image of the original wave, which he calls the "complex conjugate."

> As Cramer explains it, when the future-generated conjugate propagates back through time to [meet] the origin of the quantum wave itself...the two waves multiply [in space and time] and the result is the creation of the probability-curve for the event occurring in space and time.

> Cramer calls the original wave an "offer" wave, the conjugate wave an "echo" wave, and the multiplication of the two a "transaction"...an offer wave is sent to a receiver. The receiver accepts the offer and sends confirmation back along the same line...

> Every observation is both the start of a wave propagating toward the future in search of a receiver-event and itself the receiver of a wave that propagated towards it from some past event...every observation—every act of conscious awareness—sends out both a wave toward the future and a wave toward the past...

> Which future event sends back the echo wave? Cramer believes that only one future does this—the one producing the echo that happens to have the best chance of forming a successful transaction with the present.[16]

Whereas, Cramer believes that the only future that sends back the echo wave is the one that has the best chance of connecting with the present, Wolf's view is in line with the Many Worlds Interpretation of Quantum Mechanics, in that it is not just the best-chance future but rather an infinity of futures (a.k.a. parallel worlds) which each contain a single future event that connect with the present event through the modulation effect (modulation is the product of the multiplication of two waves). Once the modulation takes place, the parallel worlds split off and no longer interfere with each other.

Wolf's elaboration on Cramer's theory is to say that the primary function of the mind is that of converting possibility-waves into probability-curves by performing this squaring operation, thus producing probabilistic outcomes in the real world.

Other physicists like Dr. David Albert of Columbia University think this is a totally anthropomorphic view of quantum physics.

Dr. David Albert maintains that superposition is even stranger than all of the above postulations can even hint at; that all these theories are coming from our current mind-set in an attempt to make sense out of something that cannot be made sensible. "It's rather that the particle is in situation in which questions about its position can't even be raised," says Albert, "in which questions about its position don't even make sense, in which asking about the particle's position has the same logical status as asking about the political affiliations of a tuna sandwich like I said, or the marital status of the number five."[17]

Bottom line, folks: it's all a matter of interpretation!

8

THE MAGIC OF *THE SECRET*

"Individuals of true power typically have more of the things that misguided thinkers believe cause internal conflict (money, sex, food, power), and yet, for some strange reason... **they're not troubled...and they suffer no internal conflicts.**"[1]

James Arthur Ray
Thought Leader

Of the numerous teachers who are featured in *The Secret*, there are a few whose inclinations and methods veer more towards the mystical and the magical than the rest of their peers in the movie/book, including the following:

James Arthur Ray's Journey of Power®

President and CEO of Carlsbad, California-based James Ray International, he spends over 200 days a year at public appearances and seminars, teaching his trademarked Journey of Power® experience, which is "a fusion of wealth-building principles, success strategies, and the teachings of all great spiritual traditions, mystery schools, and esoteric studies that he has experienced and assimilated over the last twenty-five years."[2] The Journey of Power® program essentially shows participants how to bridge the gap between real-world success and spiritual fulfillment.

His prior experience included five years as a sales manager with AT&T and four years as a "personal and business growth expert" at AT&T's National Education Center and the AT&T School of Business. In 1991, he started working with bestselling author (*The 7 Habits of Highly Effective People*) Steven Covey's Covey Leadership Center, teaching business leaders in Fortune 500 companies.

In 1992, Ray formed Quantum Consulting Group, attracting large corporate clients such as Boeing Aircraft, Tropicana, and AT&T, later forming his current company James Ray International.

Ray has been extremely successful at marketing his company's seminars. In addition to the Journey of Power®, he has also trademarked Harmonic Wealth®, described as "what can be achieved when five key areas of life are in harmony with one another: financial, relational, intellectual, physical, and spiritual," and Entrepreneurial Mindset® (Ray often refers to himself as the "The Master of The Entrepreneurial Mindset®").

According to the website of Speakers' bureau Keynote Speakers, Inc., Ray charges $25-40,000 to give a lecture, offering such speech titles as "Harmonic Wealth" and "Turn Your Company Into a Raging, Profit Producing Machine."[3] Of course it's likely that his fees are now significantly higher, in the wake of *The Secret*'s success.

He is the author of several books including *The Science of Success: How to Attract Prosperity* and *Create Harmonic Wealth Through Proven Principles and Practical Spirituality: How to Use Spiritual Power to Create Tangible Results* and a DVD, *Quantum Creations: Create Wealth in All Areas of Your Life...*

As just a taste of Ray's teachings, consider a topic he frequently lectures on:

Seven Secrets of Top Performers

1) High achievers know exactly what they want.

2) Top performers visualize themselves in possession of their desired results.

3) Highly successful people have an unbending belief in themselves and their abilities.

4) Achievers take action "as if" they were already in possession of the goal they desire.

5) Winners take full responsibility for their own destiny.

6) Top performers build high-leveraged partnerships.

7) Great achievers are great givers.[4]

Ray's website offers several free resources and many courses, books, CDs and DVDs for sale. Indeed, as with all of the teachers in this chapter, the product Ray sells is the dream of commercial success which has many of the critics of *The Secret* (who are multiplying in direct proportion to the increasing success of the book and film) furious about the overt materialism of Byrne and her teachers.

Mr. Magick

Ray's chief distinction among his peers in *The Secret* is his very public embrace of mysticism and the occult. More on his views can be seen on his IBIS[5] website, where you can learn about his courses on Modern Magick and his IBIS spiritual movement that draws on transpersonal, esoteric and shamanic traditions, both modern and ancient, that are meant to deepen the participants' personal relationships with their "Creative Source."

In medieval times, of course, such activities would have unleashed ingeniously elaborate desecrations of each participant's anatomical parts. Luckily for Ray and the rest of us, those dark days are over!

Ray's detractors are not the usual polite handwringers we've seen: those with genuine concern for the innocent souls being misled by *The Secret*. Ray's nemeses, rather, are Christian rabble-rousers of a different stripe, with an angry streak and a particular obsession with a so-called "Rosicrucian"/"Masonic" conspiracy which looms in the shadows, quietly slinking into our TV sets, our movie theaters and magazine racks, from the pierced bellyrings of nubile popstars to the self-help messages of such films as *The Secret*. The ultimate aim of the nefarious "Rosicrucian" plot is to destroy all Christian decency before taking over the world with a global, godless, sexually profligate, fascist dictatorship, à la George Orwell's *1984*.

Therefore, it was hardly surprising to find the following posts on the über-conservative chatboard, "Free Republic," soon after *The Secret* appeared on Oprah:

New Spiritual Method Called 'The Secret' Promoted On TV Has A Hidden Occult Link

Posted on 02/19/2007 12:42:01 PM PST by Coleus:

We have to issue an occult watch—perhaps "warning" is more like it—for a new self-help trend that apparently is sweeping or beginning to sweep segments of America. The "method" is now on DVD as a movie called *The Secret*, and has been featured, among other places, on *Oprah* and *Larry King Live*....

Due to the power of the Winfrey show, and previous complaints of flirtation with the New Age, we recommend that Christians stay away from this "method" and even the movie...[6]

Posted on 02/19/2007 7:53:59 PM PST by Gal.5:1 (stand firm, speak truth in love):

The Secret: ...*The Secret* teachers are not followers of Jesus Christ and have rejected the God of the Bible, and the truth of God's word, and have rejected faith in His Son, Jesus. They have fashioned a system of personal power, based on human power. This philosophy and method is just the doorway/lowest level of the world of deep occultic mystery religion, which is the belief that either lucifer is god, or "we are god"...This is satan's religion; it is very popular... Those who pervert true Biblical faith make it about what we want, when true Biblical faith is about what God wants, and our faith and trust in Him, and obeying Him because of our love for Him, and because He is God... God has openly revealed all truth that we need, and He has not kept it a secret. **Secret philosophies that come from the world of occult and sorcery have been keeping these philosophies secret for a long time, but now they are beginning to introduce them to the general public, because the whole world is being prepared for Antichrist.**[7]

IBIS & Modern Magick™

According to Ray, the Institute of Balanced and Integrated Spirituality is the result of more than two decades that he devoted to the immersive study of the world's great esoteric disciplines, from the shamans of the Andes and the Amazon, to the mystery schools of Egypt, to the teachers in far-flung spots in the South Pacific. There were many times when he was extremely uncomfortable and his life was at risk but he claims that it was all worth it. Having synthesized what he learned, he now offers the life-changing insights he gleaned from these extreme experiences in his *Modern Magick* workshops, given once a year, in Kona Hawaii for $5,695 per person.

Now I'm going to let you in on a little secret. These real life teachers, gurus and shamans are not the meek, mild, mousy people you might think. They have thunderous personalities and were some of the wildest, most interesting characters I've ever met.

The belief that to be spiritual we must be meek and mild and talk in a harmonious whisper is a bunch of baloney...

Individuals of true power typically have more of the things that misguided thinkers believe cause internal conflict (money, sex, food, power), and yet, for some strange reason...

...they're not troubled...and they suffer no internal conflicts.

This is why they're really fun to be around. They have so much in their life, they're joyous about it, and when in their presence...things light up![8]

Ray's Theory about "Ascenders" and "Descenders"

Ray's theory about "Ascenders" and "Descenders" would surely make the Freeper chatboard posters' heads spin!

[The] ascenders want to get the hell out of here, and on the opposite end of the spectrum, we have the "descenders..." The descending mentality believes that everything to do with Earth is spiritual and sacred, and anything that denies these things is "sin."

...The descending approach has most often been pegged by the ascenders as "pagan," which really translates to mean "anything that doesn't agree with us."

Check around, and you'll notice increasing numbers of Shamanic teachings, Native American and indigenous events, Wicca workshops and many others. These traditions embrace and celebrate the physical journey and the joys of Earth.[9]

Joe Vitale: "Mr. Fire"

"Mr. Fire" is the highly-prolific author of the international bestsellers, *The Attractor Factor* (which, at one point, beat *Harry Potter*), *The Greatest Money-Making Secret in History!*, *Life's Missing Instruction Manual* (which was a number one bestselling book), the number one bestselling *Nightingale-Conant* audio program, *The Power of Outrageous Marketing*, and numerous other works. He also wrote a business book on circus showman P.T. Barnum, *There's a Customer Born Every Minute*. His most recent books are *Zero Limits: The Secret Hawaiian System for Wealth, Health, Peace and More*, *Hypnotic Writing*, and *Buying Trances: A New Psychology of Sales and Marketing*. His next book, to be published by John Wiley and Sons, is titled *The Key: The Missing Secret for Attracting Whatever*

You Want. He has several more marketing books coming out in 2008, including *Inspired Marketing, Your Internet Cash Machine,* and *The Seven Lost Secrets of Success.*

I'd say he's on fire, alright!!!

Much of Vitale's work (and arguably, of his success) is based on his skills with hypnotherapy. He is a certified hypnotherapist, a certified metaphysical practitioner, a certified Chi Kung healer, an ordained minister and holds doctorate degrees in Metaphysical Science and Marketing, all of which come in handy at his positions as President of Hypnotic Marketing, Inc. and at Frontier Nutritional Research, Inc., both based outside of Austin, Texas.

Vitale claims to be the world's first hypnotic writer and has created software such as the Hypnotic Writing Wizard, plus he has a Miracles Coaching program and is a frequent public speaker.

As a fun side project, "Mr. Fire" helped create the world's first healthy margarita mix, called Fit-A-Rita™!

Joe Vitale is a personal friend of Dr. Ihaleakala Hew Len, the Hawaiian therapist who allegedly healed an entire ward of criminally insane people at the Hawaiian State Hospital, back in the 1980s.[10] Dr. Hew Len did this by using the updated Ho'oponopono method he learned from Morrnah Simeona a Kahuna from Hawaii over 20 years ago. The book, *Zero Limits*, that became a bestseller at Amazon before it was released in July 2007, is about Joe Vitale's (as well as others') journey with this unusual method of healing learned from Dr. Ihaleakala Hew Len.

Mike Dooley: King TUT

Unlike many of his peer teachers, Dooley isn't a wealth coach, although he has a financial/accounting background that is way more impressive than many of those coaches, having worked for international consulting/accounting colossus PriceWaterhouse for many years. In 1989 he started TUT® (Totally Unique Thoughts®) with his brother and mother. It was essentially a t-shirt business and it took off to the extent that they were carried in outlets as large as Macy's and Disney World as well as their own stores. They claim to have sold over a million t-shirts by the time they closed their last store ten years later. As Dooley relates on his company website,

> After graduating with a degree in accounting I joined the most prestigious of the then "Big Eight" accounting firms. Before long I was "selectively transferred" into their exclusive tax department (that's a doozy of a story you can hear about in my audio recordings!), which led to my acceptance of a "tour of duty" in Riyadh, Saudi Arabia. From Riyadh, I traveled extensively around the world, fulfilling a

goal with uncanny accuracy, that I had written down less than 2 years earlier; in my travels I visited 17 countries, most in Africa, Asia and the Far East, and I remember being blown away by my surroundings one morning during breakfast at the Regent Hotel in Kowloon, overlooking the island of Hong Kong—realizing how I had visualized the exact same "picture," hardly 24 months earlier, based on a glossy advertisement in a magazine like *Architectural Digest*.

When the tour in Riyadh was complete I chose to repatriate in Boston where I continued excelling in the firm's international tax department. I stayed there for almost 2 years before deciding it was time to try some new challenges. To be closer to family I moved to Orlando, Florida, and from there I decided to pursue another dream, starting my own company. Only problem was...I had no idea what kind of company I wanted to own, or where to begin.

Within a few months I joined talents with those of my artistic brother, and managerial mother, and we launched, from scratch, TUT®, Totally Unique T-shirts®. One million T's, 3 books, and an audio program later, TUT® has evolved into today's Totally Unique Thoughts® and the web site now before you.[11]

The website before you, should you navigate in that direction, is TUT's Adventurers Club, which describes itself as a place for "like minded 'thinkers' from around the world who believe that living within the jungles of space and time, as a creation amongst our creations, is the ultimate Adventure, because thoughts become things, and dreams come true." There are email newsletters, forums and all the other "community" functions common on websites looking to attract repeat and interactive visitors. Offline, TUT promotes events that Mike Dooley speaks at, cruises, and promises eventual local chapter meetings. They claim over 130,000 members from over 174 countries.

But apparently it wasn't such a smooth transition from selling T-shirts to launching an online motivation business. Remember that the Dooleys launched their site right at the peak of the dotcom boom, and just before the subsequent crash in 2001. Dooley wrote in 2003:

> If ever there was proof of magic in my life, that I now spend part of every day writing for "the Universe," is it. Not even four short years ago, after we closed down the last of the TUT stores and liquidated our remaining inventory, I briefly hit the pavement with my accountant's resume in hand.
>
> Fortunately, no one was hiring (at least not me!), and fortunately again, I had enough money from our T-shirt days to coast awhile. Even more fortunately, I still had a thousand or so people looking forward to receiving my "Monday Morning Motivators" via email each week.

So I decided that as long as I didn't have to work, yet, I'd keep doing the one thing that filled me with the greatest sense of accomplishment and purpose—write. And figure out how to make it pay, later.[12]

Luckily (or was it the Law of Attraction?) for Dooley, his writings and his site found an audience and presumably he now makes a reasonable living from it.

Every member of the TUT site (they call them Adventurers) is required to take this "oath":

> In the face of adversity, uncertainty and conflicting sensory information, I hereby pledge to remain ever mindful of the magical, infinite, loving reality I live in. A reality that conspires tirelessly in my favor. I further recognize, that living within space and time, as a Creation amongst my Creations, is the ultimate Adventure, because thoughts become things, dreams come true, and all things remain forever possible. As a Being of Light, I hereby resolve to live, love and be happy, at all costs, no matter what, with reverence and kindness for All. So be it!

TUT's site is refreshingly less commercial than the websites of many of Dooley's fellow *Secret* teachers, although it does offer a couple of his books and Dooley's twelve-hour audio CD set called "Infinite Possibilities: The Art of Living Your Dreams":

BEYOND THE SECRET

It's perhaps a reminder of what lies in store for each one of us, every minute of every day, and by keeping it in mind, it forces us to remember the bigger picture, the magic behind reality, and the fact that we are never as trapped, limited, or lost as we sometimes fear. It's too easy to fall prey to negative thinking when we become obsessed with our past or overwhelmed by the conditions presently before us, and then worse, we begin to program our futures, based on the very unfavorable conditions we've been focusing on.

"Infinite Possibilities" is a reminder that our life, and our fortunes, can radically change for the better, on a dime.[13]

Raised as a Catholic, Dooley is a very intuitive person. He claims to read very few books, maybe one or two a year, although the few that he has read have been very influential. As a child he taught himself hypnosis from several books and as a teen he was enthralled by *The Inner Game of Tennis* (W. Timothy Gallwey) and *Psycho-Cybernetics* (Maxwell Maltz). In college, he read and was greatly influenced by *The Silva Mind Control Method* by José Silva and the *Seth* series of books by Jane Roberts. He says,

With my own inner search no longer lost in space I began to use and apply the understandings that were solidified by the Seth Material without any looking back. With the answers to my fundamental questions revealed, the focus of my life has become the application, or the living, of the truths I've found—a mighty tall, but rewarding, order. Today it's through the pursuit of my goals and dreams that I learn my lessons and even greater secrets about life and myself.[14]

At the end of his *Weight Watchers* interview, editor Emma Clayton asks Dooley what he would tell people to motivate and inspire them. He responds,

For inspiration, I don't think anything works quite as well as a heavy dose of truth, so I'll leave each of your readers with this: "You live in a Universe that adores you, a Universe with inviolate principles that anyone can harness without limitations or regard to their past, and one in which dream manifestation is inevitable once you truly understand the nature of your reality and your divine heritage.

You can do no wrong, you've made no mistakes, and even now as you read these words, you are bathed in infinite love. All is well."[15]

Marie Diamond: Move Your Couch and Get Rich!

For twenty years, Marie Diamond has been practicing Feng Shui, refining the knowledge given to her at an early age. She is now an internationally known master and the Feng Shui specialist and Chinese astrologer for Tarot.com and Aol.com. I am grouping her together with the more magically-oriented speakers because Feng Shui can seem to be a kind of magic, to Westerners.

Born in Belgium, she was trained as a lawyer and criminologist and worked for the Belgian and European governments and then as a project manager for a multinational publishing company. Marie moved to the United States five years ago and has since connected with numerous Hollywood celebrities, major film directors and producers, music giants, and famous authors, including our favorite *Secret* teacher, Jack Canfield of *Chicken Soup for the Soul* fame. She is also part of Canfield's Transformational Leadership Council, which includes Bill Harris, John Gray, John Assaraf, DC Cordova, Paul Scheele, and many others.

It will come as no surprise by now that Ms. Diamond offers personal coaching and a variety of seminars, courses and products for sale. For instance, she offers a series of classes called Inner Diamond Feng Shui:

> Techniques are provided that quickly release old, unwanted emotional and mental patterns that block access to the gifts and abundance of the universe. As we become proficient at releasing our blocks, we also learn how to use the Law of Attraction. The Law of Attraction is a universal law that brings

supportive people into our lives as well as healthier relationships, work that is in alignment with our life's purpose and more peace, happiness and abundance on all levels.[16]

Diamond has her own spin on the Law of Attraction, based on her studies of the ancient Chinese philosophy of Feng Shui:

You and your home are one unified field, one quantum field of unlimited possibilities. What is in you aligns with what is outside of you. The first thing you align with is your home or office. You can start with your transformation of your mind, feelings and actions and it will manifest in your home and office. But if you don't adapt your environment, the universe will receive a mixed message from you.

When you adapt your home and office to your wishes for success, abundance, good health, romance and enlightened wisdom, the universe will support you in a fast easy flow of manifestation.[17]

9

CHRISTIANITY & *THE SECRET*

"The teachings of *The Secret*
are not only false;
they are spiritually dangerous."[1]

Kerby Anderson
National Director, Probe Ministries

A question that often comes up in TV interviews with *The Secret*'s featured speakers is whether their teachings conflict with Christianity. Lisa Nichols deftly skirted around this issue on *Larry King Live*:

KING: You have strong Christian faith. Does [*The Secret*] conflict with this?

NICHOLS: No, for me it doesn't because I searched this to make sure that God was all through it. I mean, my commitment to God is stronger than anything.[2]

Notice that it was King who called Nichols a "Christian" and that her reply that her "commitment to God is stronger than anything"—not her commitment to Christ.

The simple truth is that the "All is One," monistic worldview espoused in the film and the book runs 180° counter to the teachings of the Christian church. As a result, *The Secret* has raised the hackles of fundamentalist watchdogs:

> Of the twenty-four *Secret* teachers, perhaps the most troubling is Rev. Michael Bernard Beckwith...His message is that we are co-creators with God and that our abilities are unlimited. Our potential is divine in nature. Dr. Beckwith is troubling, in my view, because he represents a pseudo-Christianity. He has the greatest ability to be used to deceive those whom God has touched by His Gospel. The Christian who is unable to rightly discern God's Word will fall prey to such false teaching as found in *The Secret*...[3]

Lisa Nichols, like Beckwith and some 95% of the other teachers who appear in *The Secret*, makes routine appearances at Unity churches around America.

The Unity Church

As I've mentioned previously, *The Secret* movie and book are de facto vehicles for the teachings of the Unity Church, whose followers consider themselves to be "positive" Christians, using the Christian Bible as their central text. However, Unity's basic tenets that God is a universal presence and that divinity exists in all people are contrary to mainstream Christian faith. Unity teachings are based on five basic principles:

1) God is the source and creator of all. There is no other enduring power. God is good and present everywhere.

2) We are spiritual beings, created in God's image. The spirit of God lives within each person; therefore, all people are inherently good.

3) We create our life experiences through our way of thinking.

4) There is power in affirmative prayer, which we believe increases our connection to God.

5) Knowledge of these spiritual principles is not enough. We must live them.[4]

Neale Donald Walsch & His *Conversations with God*

Neale Donald Walsch is a novelist and author of the fabulously successful book series, *Conversations with God*. In addition to the *Conversations* series (three books so far), he has authored *Friendship with God, Communion with God, The New Revelations, Tomorrow's God, What God Wants* and most recently, *Home with God: In a Life That Never Ends.*

Born in 1943 in Milwaukee, Wisconsin, he was raised as a Roman Catholic, but found himself reaching out for what he terms a "New Spirituality." According to his official biography, his *Conversations with God* series of books "redefined God and shifted spiritual paradigms around the globe."[5] It's hard to know quite what to say to that! But Walsch does his best to explain in an interview with *Share Guide*'s Dennis Hughes:

> I think the new spirituality will be a spirituality that's not based on a particular dogma. And that steps away from the old spiritual paradigm that we have created on this planet, which comes from a thought that there is such a thing as being better. The sad part about our past is that religions, ironically enough, are responsible for creating the most destructive idea that has ever been visited upon the human race: the idea that there is such a thing as "better." I question that the word better has any real value as it's used by many religions—and then subsequently by other institutions in our society.[6]

Before publishing these books in the early 1990s, Walsch suffered a series of crushing blows—a fire that destroyed all of his belongings, the break-up of his marriage, a car accident that left him with a broken neck. Once recovered but alone and unemployed, Walsch was forced to live in a tent in Jackson Hot Springs, just outside Ashland, Oregon, collecting and recycling aluminum cans in order to eat. At the time, Walsch thought his life had come to an end. Despondent, Walsch began his writings after working his way out of homelessness, following a short-lived job as a radio talk show host.[7]

Obviously, the success of his first book has been transformational. In addition to his thriving spiritual book line, he has an online course business and holds "retreats" around the world (and on cruise ships) throughout the year. He lives with his wife, Nancy, at a retreat site in Ashland, Oregon, where they run The ReCreation Foundation, Inc. also known as The Conversations with God Foundation. (Walsch has met with some criticism for what some see as appearing overly zealous in finding ways to make money for his spin-off organizations.)

Asked whether or not the success surprised him, Walsch answered:

> Well, yes and no. If I could give that kind of an answer. Yes, I think it did surprise me at one level and at another level, when I thought about it more than 20 seconds, I realized that if in fact it was God's intention for this book to touch the world, then it wouldn't surprise me at all, it shouldn't, that it has become such an instant success. And so, yes and no. I think that from a limited physical perspective that I

sometimes hold as the personality known as Neale, I was a bit shocked at both the speed and the enormity of its success but from a higher level, when I move to my own highest place of being-ness, I see that it is all perfectly natural and normal for this outcome to have occurred, and for it not to have occurred would have been the surprising thing given God's intentions in the matter.[8]

He says that his books are not channeled, rather that they are inspired by God and that they can help a person relate to Him from a modern perspective. The God in his books, for example, says that "there is nothing you have to do." Walsch believes in a pantheistic God who tries to communicate Himself as being unselfish (pantheism literally means "All is God"). His expressed vision is of a New Spirituality: an expansion and unification of all present theologies; a refreshing of them, rendering all of our current sacred teachings even more relevant to our present day and time. He created Humanity's Team as a spiritual movement whose purpose is to communicate and implement New Spirituality beliefs, particularly that we are all one with God and one with life, in a shared global state of being. There are parallels with this philosophy and that of the Bahá'í Faith, although the latter is not monist. Also, there are similarities with the very early Gnosticism.

Walsch starred in the 2003 New Age movie *Indigo*, which he wrote with James Twyman, dealing with the redemption of a grandfather (Walsch) through his granddaughter, an indigo child.[9] Apparently he's got the movie bug, and his character is the lead role (played by Canadian actor Henry Czerny) in *Conversations With God: The Movie* (2006), the story of a down-and-out man who inadvertently becomes a spiritual messenger and bestselling author (sound familiar?).

Walsch's views are generally in alignment with those of the Unity Church and he speaks regularly at Unity Churches throughout the United States. To Unity followers, the universe and "God" are one, which is a foundational tenet of Eastern religious philosophies.

Prior to founding his Unity church in 1889, Charles Fillmore studied Hinduism, Buddhism, Hermeticism, Rosicrucianism and Theosophy and the influence of these philosophies on his church is not merely evident but embraced. The Unity followers' belief in reincarnation, as well as their monistic view that "All is One," has caused some Christian theologians to describe Unity as an offshoot of Hinduism. Other Christians are less charitable:

> [A] characteristic of cults that is true of Unity is the denial of the biblical doctrine of salvation by faith in Christ's person and His finished work on the cross. In Unity, salvation comes by recognizing our inherent divinity and our oneness with God.

Unity is, in my opinion, the most deceptive of the cultic groups that use the word Christian in their name. Unity's distinction is that the follower of its teaching is encouraged to remain in his respective church home whether it be Baptist, Methodist, Presbyterian, or whatever. The followers of Unity consider their denominational affiliation as a mission field where they can subtly disseminate their ideas...

Unity is not based on biblical teaching. To the contrary, it is heavily influenced by Eastern thought and belief. Unity is a classic New Age cult and is not Christian in any aspect of its doctrine or teaching.[10]

Dogma and Demons

Christian fundamentalists believe that the Unity teachings are inherently Satanic because they instruct followers to see God in all things. Fundamentalists believe that meditation and creative visualization put their practitioners in jeopardy of summoning demons. (To be fair, meditators of all kinds, from Buddhists to occult practitioners have long warned of this danger to neophytes...)

When you enter the realm of spiritual discovery through meditative practices or some other psycho-spiritual methodology you will at some point find yourself face to face with a demon masquerading as your inner guide or Master Teacher. It is instructive to note that this inner guide or spirit guide will at some point in time bring you an urgent message from the "other side." The subtle deception that lies in wait for its innocent prey is not discriminating. It will consume whomever it finds to seduce.[11]

The New Thought movement grew as a revolt against what its founders viewed to be the negative dogmas in the churches of the mid-19th Century and it was driven by their observation that physical healing could often be achieved through the power of mind and spiritual awareness.

As that initial idea unfolded into successful application, practitioners of New Thought began to see that the power of an uplifted consciousness could also bring healing to negative circumstances and conditions in one's personal life. As it evolves today, twenty-first century New Thought is driven by a far broader intention. Planetary healing through self-realization is emerging as the new promise of these teachings.[12]

God and Creation:
A Catholic Perspective

While attending an Irish wake recently, in a backyard in Darien, Connecticut, I had the unprecedented occasion to casually converse with a Catholic priest, a beautiful and charming man in his late fifties. True to Irish tradition, the party was fairly raucous, in celebration of the life of my friend's great aunt. Amid this scene, he asked me what I did for a living. I told him that I'd just written a book about the lifeworks of several quantum physicists.[13] He asked me to briefly explain some of their theories and after I did, I asked him to explain the Christian view of how reality works.

He explained that Christians believe that God created the universe and that He set it in motion but He remains separate from the universe. The priest likened God's relationship to His Creation to an author's relationship to her book; the book is *not* the author just as God is *not* the universe.

What this said to me was that from a Christian perspective, the universe as a whole does not exist and "All is *not* One." There was no sense in my debating with this very pleasant man, clearly committed to his faith, all dressed in black with a Roman collar.

Our conversation shifted to how upset he was over the recent order by the Supreme Court of his home state of Massachusetts to legalize gay marriage. He was upset that this had passed into state law, without a referendum allowing the people to vote on it. I opined that Massachusetts was one of the few places in America where there was the highest likelihood that people would vote "yes" to gay marriage, if given the chance. He chuckled and half agreed...

The Prayer of Jabez: *The Secret*, Christian-Style?

The bestselling *Prayer of Jabez* Christian book series by "Promise Keeper" stadium speaker, Dr. Bruce H. Wilkinson represents a possible bridge between Christian fundamentalism and secular self-help. Wilkinson's teachings are similar in essence to *The Secret*'s. Apparently, this is the kind of message that people want to hear, as his first *Prayer of Jabez* book sold almost 8 million copies within a year of release.

Jabez is an Old Testament character whose short prayer punctuates the litany of "begats" in the Levite genealogy in the Book of Chronicles:

> And Jabez called on the God of Israel saying, "Oh, that you would bless me indeed, and enlarge my territory, that your hand would be with me, and that you would keep me from evil, that I may not cause pain."
>
> So God granted him what he requested.
>
> —*I Chronicles 4:10 NKJV*[14]

Wilkinson calls Jabez "a daring prayer that God always answers," and he encourages readers to pray it for at least thirty days, in order to see results. The *Jabez* series engages the average Christian American with an everyday, commercial language, seemingly modeled on Jack Canfield's *Chicken Soup for the Soul* series.

When was the last time God worked through you in such a way that you knew beyond doubt that God had done it? In fact, when was the last time you saw miracles happen on a regular basis in *your* life? If you're like most believers I've met, you wouldn't know how to ask for that kind of experience, or even if you should...Because you're reading this book, I believe you share my desire to reach for a life that will be "more honorable" for God. Not that you should wish others to reach for less, but for you, nothing but God's fullest blessing will do...God really does have unclaimed blessings waiting for you, my friend. I know it sounds impossible—even embarrassingly suspicious in our self-serving day. Yet that very exchange—your want for God's plenty—has been His loving will for you from eternity past. And with a handful of core commitments on your part, you can proceed from this day forward with the confidence and the expectation that your heavenly Father will bring it to pass for you.[15]

Although Wilkinson has devoted his life to teaching evangelical Christian biblical doctrine, even he has met with reproach from hard line fundamentalists...

Reverend James Mulholland recently wrote a book on the Lord's Prayer in response to the Jabez phenomenon. He says the two prayers offer a sharp contrast: Jesus praying for God's will versus Jabez praying for himself.[16]

The bottom line is, fundamentalist Christian teaching is incompatible with the teachings of both the *Prayer of Jabez* and *The Secret*.

10

THE LAW OF ATTRACTION DEBATE

"The Law of Attraction" is true—as far as it goes. The problem is that *The Secret* takes this one relatively small piece of the puzzle and makes it the entire puzzle."

Ken Wilber's
Integral Naked newsletter

Bob Doyle & *Wealth Beyond Reason*

D oyle's a bit different from most of the success coaches featured in *The Secret*. For one thing, he hasn't been doing it all that long. Probably the best way to get a sense of this is to quote him on his personal story:

> In 2002, I was in my fourth year at a corporate job which I had grown to absolutely hate. There was no sense of purpose or passion in the work I was

doing, and I absolutely knew that there was more to life than a nice paycheck—which I did have at that time. Of course, it was that paycheck which kept me "enslaved" in that job because I felt I needed the security it provided.

But inside, I was dying. It literally felt like that. I would sit at that desk and feel like my spirit was literally drying up.

So, in January of 2002, I simply quit my job. No safety net whatsoever. Obviously, that's not the correct step for everyone, and things were certainly tough as a result, but I would die if I stayed. There was no question in my mind...

Long story short (if possible), I was actually out "on the road" talking to people about what I'd learned about "creating your own reality," at that time focusing on manifestation through meditation.

But there was a HUGE piece missing. Although I understood these principles on an intellectual level for the most part, what I did NOT fully understand was the Law of Attraction, and how it really works, and primarily how it was working in my own life.

The fallout from having that piece missing was a DISASTROUS financial situation. While I'm happy to say that I never had to declare bankruptcy, I'm sure there would have been those who would have advised it. We had less than no money, and things were getting stressful to say the least.

At that point—luckily—I had learned enough to recognize that I was trying to figure everything out for myself, rather than truly allowing the Universe to handle all this for me—something that I "taught" folks to do, but obviously hadn't followed myself.

The day came that I just gave up "trying," and in essence asked the Universe for direction, and committed to following my intuition without question, regardless of how far "off path" the signs I got seemed to take me. I simply trusted, and let go of having to have all the answers myself.

Through an amazing series of seemingly unrelated situations, I attracted the information that changed my life forever. Information that opened my eyes to what I'd been missing the whole time. It was information that explained HOW all this stuff I talked about actually worked—at the scientific level—so that any lingering resistance I had to FULLY incorporating into my life disappeared.[1]

He considers himself to be a "Law of Attraction Coach" and has authored a self-help book containing his prescription for prosperity: *Wealth Beyond Reason: Your Complete Handbook For Boundless Living*.[2]

Doyle expounds tirelessly on the LOA in his book and at his website, where he offers an online course of the same name. A quick sampling:

> To attract wealth, you first have to BE wealthy. THEN, you think wealthy thoughts, speak wealthy affirmations, and take wealthy action...

> A truly wealthy person isn't wealthy because they have money. They have money, because they are wealthy! That's the distinction that most people have backward!

> ...again, Wealth is a decision. If you aren't currently experiencing wealth, you first need to realize that abundance is everywhere...in fact it's all there is. Poverty and lack are the illusions. You can shift your consciousness to Wealth—BE Wealth—by simply making the decision, THEN your thoughts, speech, and action will allow you to experience the wealth that is yours![3]

Doyle tries to avoid sounding too "New Agey," stating right up front in the introduction to his book that he needs to deliver his message in a way "that does not seem 'hocus-pocus' or require you to adopt some kind of 'new-age' belief system, because I would lose a great many of those I am trying to reach if I went that route."

Undoubtedly he's right.

New Age Guilt: Does Everyone Really Create Their Own Reality?

For at least a decade, The Prophets Conference has been promoting speaking tours featuring alternative thinkers, healers, spiritual figures and, more recently, some of the people, like Bob Doyle, who appeared in *The Secret*. On June 27, 2007 holistic writer William Bloom, who was about to appear at a Prophets Conference event in the UK, wrote a mass email to the subscribers of the Prophets Conference list, titled: "Does Everyone Really Create Their Own Reality?" where he mused about the tragedies that befall people on a regular basis, the life lessons these contain and the strange brew of "New Age guilt" that can accompany the reactions to these unfortunate events. He had especially strong words for the New Age community:

> Over the years it has been an honor for me to advance and defend new age and holistic spirituality. I love its open-mindedness, its embrace of metaphysics and the way it combines spiritual work with healthcare. But I have also despaired at times about its apparent lack of morality and compassion when faced with the realities of people's suffering.
>
> This coldness is often explained away with half-baked ideas about how energies, karma and the laws of attraction work. These often reach a peak of disturbing smugness when a new age "philosopher"

faced with cruel suffering says authoritatively: "People create their own reality" or "Their soul chose it—its their karma" or "Everything is perfect in God's Plan—you just need to perceive it differently." People who say such things seem to have no idea how smug and nasty they sound. Nor of the hurt they cause.

Bloom then goes on to describe the infernal situations being played out daily in Darfur and elsewhere in Africa:

These minor examples of personal distress are nothing compared to the more dramatic tragedies being endured on the world stage. What follows is recent testimony from a woman at the center of the Darfur crisis (*New Internationalist*, June 2007):

"My baby boy was thrown on the fire in front of me. My daughter was older. They thought she was a boy so they slaughtered her too—they snapped the neck like a chicken. Some of the children they threw down as well...After they raped the women they cut off their breasts to make them suffer. They used those of us who were left as donkeys."

...Surely all this suffering can only be approached with stillness, humility and wisdom of the heart. Not with half-baked metaphysics and denial. It is pure ignorance, shameful and cold-hearted emotional cruelty to suggest that these women and children asked for this destiny, deserved it, chose it or created their own reality. It completely misunderstands karma and the laws of attraction.

There is a frequent error of assuming that souls have complete control and choice over their incarnations. New souls entering for the first time, for example, may simply be drawn to where there is a newly conceived fetus. They may have no choice but to participate in the collective rhythm and cycle. There are more dynamics in incarnation than simple choice.

Equally we do not create our lives in isolation. We pass through collective historical and karmic events over which we may have little individual power. We are participants as souls and as biological creatures in a constellation of relationships that includes our species, our gender, our family, our ancestors, our ethnicity and faith. Our parents and children, for example, are within us, as we are also within them. We are not just individual souls creating our own individual lives and futures. We are also subjects of the group soul and our histories and futures are entwined. As a species we have created a shared karma of suffering, and it is as a collective that we experience, redeem and heal it. The collective affects even the most forceful individual...

It is also completely banal and naïve to suggest that everything in God's world is good and that it is all a matter of perception. Faced with the reality of a three-year old child being sexually abused, it is simply not possible to make such a statement and be moral. It is in facing reality, not denying it, being in our hearts, that we grow and become wiser.

At the same time I fully appreciate how difficult it is to be fully present to suffering. For some people it is overwhelming because it triggers their own pain. But sooner or later on the spiritual path we have to develop the courage and strength to stay stable and loving when faced with these horrors. In the words of Carl Jung: "One does not become enlightened by imagining figures of light, but by making the darkness conscious."

All my love, William[4]

The response from the Prophets Conference list was unprecedented; people replied that their burdens of guilt for all their various problems had been lifted and some wrote that they'd wept tears of joy and relief, on reading Bloom's post.

Four days later, the Prophets Conference organizers, Robin and Cody Johnson, sent a mass email to their list saying that due to the overwhelming response to Bloom's letter they were changing the title of their upcoming event, featuring Bob Doyle among others, from the "Law of Attraction Conference" into "Manifesting a Rich Life." They posted links to a series of Bob Doyle's video clips,[5] where Doyle addressed the main objections he had personally encountered to the content of the *The Secret* since its release. The second follow-up video addresses probably the toughest LOA question ever: "How do you explain when 'bad' things happen to people who should never have attracted those bad things?"

This is my rough transcript of Doyle's second video clip:

> This is a question that comes up constantly among people who are learning about the LOA. Well, what people need to understand is that the LOA isn't only about attracting things on purpose. This isn't a personal development tool that was packaged and you can use this to get what you want. It's a much bigger law than that…**we're attracting constantly, all the time; consciously and unconsciously—most of what we experience in our everyday lives is unconscious attraction**, although it's beyond the scope of this video to get into this, but we're assembling every aspect of our reality through our interpretation of the energy that is the universe around us…our shaping of the energy that we've attracted into our experience.
>
> How do we attract that energy? Well, we're in resonance with it…by default. So, how does that happen? We attract things in our life by our vibrational resonance with them and we take on resonance from our environment, for the most part, if we're not conscious that we can do whatever we want to

with our consciousness...our attitudes about money, relationships, etc. are shaped from a very early age... we take them on and we're in resonance with those thoughts and beliefs.

You didn't do that consciously...if you were born in a country that has issues with food or the economy, you're going to take with you the thought that, "where I come from, there is no food." It's a vibration that's passed on from generation to generation...it's not their fault—and this is very key to understand.

When we're saying that a person is attracting their experience, we're not saying that the person is at fault, at all. Chances are, it was a completely unconscious act...some people complain that the LOA has all these stipulations but, look, it just is what it is; it's what you're in vibrational resonance with, period. It's not a good or bad thing. The gift that we have as human beings is that if we know that we have this ability to consciously shift our vibration to be in alignment with things that we really, truly want in our lives and if we don't know that, we're just going to keep attracting more of the same things and we're going to be resonating with all sorts of things, including disease and tragedy...

How can a horrible disaster happen to a group of people, you ask, "they weren't attracting that!" Well, they were in alignment with it and I know it sounds harsh for some people to hear but it doesn't mean anything good or bad. It just means that they were there for whatever reason, they didn't know any better and that happened. There's no better answer. No one from the outside looking in can look at a person's life that was affected by a tragedy and know everything that was going on vibrationally. There's too much going on in a person...it doesn't mean they wrote it down on a list or made a vision board about it or visualized it happening or meditated on it; it happened by default.

That's why it's key to really hear what we're saying. If you can see how it's [LOA] affected your life and continues to affect your life...and understand that you can truly change your experience and your vision of reality by creating a different vibration...so you can attract different things and learn how to release that resistance...

While there's a lot in your life that's going to happen that you have no control over, because you attracted it by default, there's much that you can start doing right now that would minimize something like that happening...so when you have a sick baby, the baby is in alignment with illness for whatever reason, it just is what it is—but now, what do we do about it? What are the choices you're going to make? The LOA isn't about fair or unfair or good or bad. It just is what it is...it's not a personal development tool, it is a law of the universe that you do have some ability to interact with, to change your experience...[6]

A Conversation with Bob Doyle: The Law of Attraction and Randomness

What I have found to be objectionable about the Law of Attraction, when interpreted in the absolutist sense, is the idea that there is no chance, "no accidents." When I contacted Bob and asked him if he thought that the Law of Attraction ultimately implied that there was no such thing as randomness, he generously replied:

> **Doyle:** Chance and even randomness are terms that we use to define circumstances that we cannot possibly explain through logic or prediction, but nonetheless, energy is always responding in a predictable manner. In other words, we may not see it coming or understand it, but there is still a perfect science to it, though it is so complex that in many cases it would be impossible for us to put together all the pieces of things that were resonating in such a way that the "random" event occurs.

> **Bruce:** It sounds like you agree with some chaos theorists who believe that there is order in chaos.

In Newtonian physics, energy is predictable.

In quantum mechanics, it is generally agreed that energy behaves in a probabilistic manner that is not always predictable and is sometimes random...

Doyle: Well, oddly, I agree with this as well...but it still depends on what we're calling random. I often wonder if we were designed to see the Biggest of All Big Pictures, or if that's "beyond the scope" of the human experience.

Our perception may always be that there is true randomness in events—but it is my opinion that there is still some divine order to it. Whether we will ever prove or demonstrate that in a scientific way, I have no idea.

This reminded me of my favorite quote by Jeff Satinover, who I profiled in a previous book[7]:

Either it is absolute chance or absolute will...Both are equally mysterious as explanations go. Indeed, they are hardly even that: **They are merely terms for something beyond our ken. You might as well call it the Tao—or Ralph.**[8]

Einstein was convinced that "God does not play dice," while his colleague Niels Bohr, the Godfather of particle physics and Quantum Mechanics, is famously quoted as saying: "Einstein, stop telling God what to do."[9]

11

INTERVIEW WITH BILL HARRIS

"The majority of the 'spiritual market'
is drawn to pre-rational magic and
myth, how do you reach the small
group who are involved in genuine,
laborious, demanding, trans-rational
spiritual practice? This is very difficult,
because both markets are referred to
as 'spiritual'...and they generally
disapprove of each other..."[1]

Ken Wilber
Philosopher

I was very lucky to meet the amazing Bill Harris and some
other members of the Transformational Leadership
Council during a documentary film shoot earlier this
year. Here's a brief email chat I had with Bill, who was
profiled earlier in this book as a leader in the self-development movement and as a speaker who appeared in *The
Secret* movie/book:

The Secret

Harris: As for *The Secret*, those with any intelligence (Ken Wilber, for instance) see it as pre-conventional [i.e., primitive] magical thinking. Reality is much more mundane: when you focus on something, you get ideas about how to make it happen, you notice resources you weren't previously noticing that could help you, you develop motivation to act, you develop internal qualities you might need, such as imagination, courage, persistence, enthusiasm, and so forth. Then, you have to act in some way. And finally, your action has to create some sort of value (that is, if you want something of value in return).

The Law of Attraction

Harris: Some of Rhonda's claims are not exactly what you would call respected in the scientific community. She happened to skillfully create something that caught the imagination of all the poor souls who desperately want to believe that there is some sort of magic that will help them get what they want without actually paying the price for getting it.

Bruce: How would you define the Law of Attraction?

Harris: The Law of Attraction is nothing more than the statement that thoughts and actions have consequences. Mixed in with those consequences are other consequences created by the thoughts and actions of other people, natural events (the weather, people being born and dying, and so forth). If you focus on what you want and take action to get it, and change your actions when you need to (because of the actions of others, intervening natural events, etc.), and are persistent, there is a high probability that you will get what you want.

Bruce: When I've heard the Law of Attraction referred to in absolutist terms, I think that this serves to undermine the productive information contributed by all the speakers. "Everything happening in your life is a function of how you are vibrating." This strikes me as a completely deterministic belief. Ironically, determinism is a philosophy which runs 180° to the underlying "feel-good" vibe of *The Secret*! Moreover, an absolutist view of the Law of Attraction would seem to deny the existence of chance or randomness, which flies in the face of science. Chance is a primary fundament of science. Is science wrong?

Randomness

Harris: Clearly, there is randomness in the universe. General Systems Theory, cybernetics, non-equilibrium thermodynamics, cellular automata theory, catastrophe theory, autopoietic system theory, dynamic systems theory, and chaos theory, among others, all have proven that much of the development of the universe happens through mechanisms based on probability.

Some people who talk about the LOA are, as we have discussed, magical thinkers—pre-rational, pre-conventional thinkers don't have the mental equipment to discern how the universe works. Some of them might believe that there is no randomness in the universe.

Bruce: Well, I'm glad we agree that there is such a thing as randomness and that *The Secret* hasn't plunged everybody into a bizarre parallel universe! I started wondering if the Law of Attraction wasn't some kind of undiscovered boson or something! I was really trying to imagine what things would be like if the Law of Attraction was as potent and quantifiable as the Law of Gravity. What it looked like to me was a nightmarish Rube Goldberg cartoon or even worse; a mechanistic, closed-end, deterministic system. A gigantic jail! Knowing that chaos and randomness are real is both terrifying yet profoundly liberating...

There are those who have suggested that some people could actually be hurt by the teaching of the Law of Attraction: "About 10% of self-help books are rated by mental-health professionals as damaging. [*The Secret*] is probably one of them."[2]

Oneness

Bruce: While we were on that incredible yacht during the Make A Change® cruise, I was too caught up with dealing with the film equipment to hear most of the lecture you were giving about cultivating the non-dual mind, which sounded very interesting. Thinking in this manner seems to be a particularly difficult task for Westerners. You even mentioned how the concept of dualism is absent from some Asian languages, which I found fascinating.

Monism, i.e., the ideal that "All is One" is propagated throughout *The Secret* and it is the lynchpin of all of the other ideas espoused in that film. How do you discuss the oneness of everything when speaking to your groups?

Harris: Just look around you. It's all one big inter-connected system. Flowers can't exist without bees, or dirt, or water, or carbon dioxide, or sunlight, which requires being on a certain kind of planet a certain distance from a certain kind of star, etc., etc. We could start with you and build a similar sequence of interconnectedness. Everything depends on and is connected to everything else. This isn't metaphysical. All you have to do is look around.

Behind that, there is something that is the background to all of this—some have, in fact, called it "the ground of being." It's like the white part of the page, which has no information, but is fundamental to the book and the writing. Or, we could talk about the space that is necessary for objects to exist. There's "nothing" there, but without it, the solids couldn't exist. This is one reason why the Buddhists say "form is nothingness, nothingness is form." Form and nothingness arise together. They go together. (Remember that I said that EVERYTHING goes together, and that includes nothingness).

Finally, your mind keeps you from seeing how everything goes together, because it wants to chop everything up into separate things and events. But where does one "thing" end and another begin? (Think of the bee and the flower again—the divisions are arbitrary; it's all one thing.) Alan Watts used to say that a thing is a "think"—as much of the whole as you decided to bite off with your mind in that moment. All these divisions happen in your mind, not in reality, in the same way that the border between the US and Canada is an IMAGINARY line. The biggest illusory division is the one that allows you to create a separate you, as if Alexandra was a separate ego in a bag of skin.

One of my pet peeves (Ken Wilber agrees with this, too) is using quantum physics to prove various kinds of magic. The quantum level is the most fundamental level in the universe, but the lowest level developmentally.

The "Oneness" we're talking about happens at the highest levels of development (and well beyond pre-conventional magical thinking). Those who use physics to "prove" what they want to believe spiritually are on the wrong track and look very foolish to real scientists.

If you want more information about how this "oneness" business works, I would suggest reading *Sex, Ecology, Spiri-*

tuality by Ken Wilber,[3] or take my online courses. You can listen to a free lesson at: http://www.centerpointe.com/life/preview.

Ken's book and my course, though, are not light undertakings. The book is nearly 800 pages, and the three online courses take 18 months to complete. Both, though, are amazing.

Bruce: Bill, do you have any ideas on how to bridge the gap between the monists and the Abrahamic contingent of this planet (Christians, Jews and Muslims) who believe that God is separate from Creation and therefore, "All is NOT One" and that there is actually a set of phenomena in existence that is "NOT God?" From the standpoint of pure logic, it is impossible to conceive of such a thing as the "universe" unless you *are* a monist.

I am sure that, after several years of experience with a diverse clientele that you have found a diplomatic way to bridge the seemingly unfathomable ideological gaps that exist within your client base and it would be amazing if this were to occur on a planetary basis...Whoever could bridge the gap between the monists and the dualists would make a bazillion dollars and finally put an end to all this religious bloodshed.

Harris: I would forget about all the fundamentalists of the world. They are very confused. It's people like Wilber that actually have a clear view of what the hell is going on. I've attached a fairly easy read summary of Ken's latest book, *The Integral Vision*.[4]

Bruce: Thanks for the book! I can't wait to read it! I guess you don't get a lot of fundamentalists coming to your seminars! Maybe Esther "Abraham" Hicks was right on track when "they" said:

> You did not come here to fix a broken world. The world is not broken. You came here to live a wonderful life. And if you can learn to relax a little and let it all in, you will begin to see the universe present you with all that you have asked for.[5]

12

KEN WILBER: *THE TRICKY BUSINESS OF CREATING YOUR OWN REALITY*

"Actually, you are creating the universe moment-to-moment, but it's not the "you" that you think..."

Ken Wilber's
Integral Naked newsletter

Ken Wilber is the author of over 30 books and is one of the most important thinkers in America today. He is the founder of the Integral Institute in Boulder, Colorado, which seeks to take the best of science, engineering, spirituality, philosophy and all the greatest human endeavors and achievements and to integrate these into a solution-based worldview, and apply them to the many different kinds of problems facing the world today. "Integral" means comprehensive, inclusive, balanced, not leaving anything out.

Integral Naked

Below is an article, *The Tricky Business of Creating Your Own Reality*, that was published in the Integral Institute's online *Integral Naked* newsletter, which is an overview of a conversation Ken had with psychotherapist and yoga instructor Julian Walker about the pros and the cons of the film, *The Secret*:

...what can be so tricky when evaluating a new approach such as *The Secret*, is that at first glance it can appear fairly innocent, even if lacking any kind of critical depth. If it's helping people feel empowered and positive about their lives, what's the problem? Well, the problem is that it's not a basically solid approach with room for improvement, it's a fundamentally confused way of understanding reality that misunderstands and contorts the genuine truths that it intuits...

As with any "you create your own reality" schema, *The Secret* fails what can be called "the Auschwitz test." According to *The Secret*, everyone who was murdered at Auschwitz—or Rwanda, or Darfur—created that reality for themselves, and therefore they are to blame for their fate. For obvious reasons, this position is as unconscionable as it is untenable.

By teaching that the world quite literally revolves around you, *The Secret* encourages and entrenches narcissism. In developmental psychology, narcissism doesn't mean an unhealthy obsession with thinking only about yourself, it means you **can't** think about yourself. The capacity for self-reflexive awareness just isn't there. The entire world and everyone in it is simply an **extension** of yourself, and you are literally unable to take the perspective of another human being. This is not mystical union; this is pre-rational fusion, and without the ability to take the perspectives of other sentient beings, the entire foundation for ethics evaporates.

Actually, **you are** creating the universe moment-to-moment, but it's not the "you" that you think. According to the great contemplative traditions, every person has at least two "selves": the finite, temporal, egoic self-sense, and the infinite, transcendental, unqualifiable Self, or I-AMness. Your Self, your I-AMness, is indeed giving rise to the entire radiant Kosmos in this and every moment, but *The Secret* teaches that your **separate self** has the power to personally manifest a new car, win the lottery, or cure cancer... and this simply isn't how things work.

"The Law of Attraction" **is true**—as far as it goes. The problem is that *The Secret* takes this one relatively small piece of the puzzle and makes it the **entire** puzzle. A positive outlook **will** change your life and your intentions **will** co-create your reality, but so will brain chemistry, interior level of development, family relationships, natural disasters, cultural trends, language structure, environmental toxins, and, basically, the slings and arrows of outrageous fortune.

Developmentally, if one uses a scale ranging from **archaic** to **magic** to **mythic** to **rational** to **pluralistic** to **integral** to **super-integral**, *The Secret* teaches the magical thought structures that were humanity's leading edge several hundred thousand years ago. As Ken explains, *The Secret* encourages childlike "primary process thinking," which can be in the form of "the law of attraction" (e.g., if one black thing is bad, then all black things are bad) and "the law of contagion" (e.g., if this particular man was powerful, then a lock of his hair must be powerful too).

The importance of understanding how unconscious **psychological shadow elements** color and affect one's experience, and how *The Secret* can agitate, alienate, repress, or—perhaps even more worrisome—act on these disowned elements of consciousness.

The genesis of the **pre/trans** or **pre/post fallacy**, and how *The Secret* is a perfect example of elevating pre-rational childish impulses to trans-rational spiritual glory. Simply because both categories of experience are **non**-rational, they can easily be confused, and often are.

The extraordinary thing about this dialogue is that, for all the critiques Ken and Julian have of *The Secret*, it's not meant as a put-down or a mean-spirited attack. As evidenced by its incredible popularity, there are millions of people who are **starving** for something other than traditional religion or modern science in their search for meaning. By using an Integral Approach, one is able to look at what new offerings like *The Secret* have to bring to the table, and assess in good faith what their strengths and weaknesses really are, for the health and nourishment of every soul who dare grasp for "something more"—and for what we consider to be the **real** Secret of transformation and human happiness, we recommend an **Integral Life Practice** and an **Integral Spirituality**, bringing together Body, Mind, and Spirit, in Self, Culture, and Nature.[1]

Wilber's latest book, *The Integral Vision*, is a summary of his lifework and comes highly recommended by Bill Harris and myself.

Synthesis

So, there you have it. We've explored a full spectrum of beliefs and methods for improving human life, from those that would tell you that the best approach is attuning yourself "to the energy of who you really are," as opposed to "dabbling" in an "action-oriented...upstream, mediocre way," to the more grounded, albeit labor-intensive Integralist approach, referred to in this chapter and expounded upon at length in Wilber's many books.

I think there is some value to all the views presented here, even those of the angry fundamentalists, and I am so very grateful to have had the opportunity of studying the works of all the teachers whom I have cited.

CONCLUSION

WHY *THE SECRET* HAS BEEN SO SUCCESSFUL

"On an ethical level, *The Secret* appears deplorable. It concerns itself almost entirely with a narrow range of middle-class concerns—houses, cars and vacations, followed by health and relationships, with the rest of humanity a very distant sixth..."

Jerry Adler
Newsweek

No sooner was *The Secret* out than a tide of criticism arose commensurate with the phenomenon's success, some of it valid and some of it colored by the personal issues of each critic.

I've observed several stages in my own relationship to the content of *The Secret*, the first being total rejection, the next being to sort through what works for me and what doesn't in the methods of the featured speakers. This is where I'm at right now. The next stage would be for me to get extremely intentional about putting what I have learned into practice and—voilà! Become "successful"!

Many people never get past the rejection stage. They just love to rant about *The Secret*'s vileness. It's actually very funny. My British niece emailed me, "I have never heard of *The Secret*...maybe it wasn't such a big thing in England! I am told it is a self-help book, which made a lot of money! I hate self-help. I think far too many people have an over-inflated sense of self nowadays! I hope the book is going along nicely though!"

I jokingly replied: "Yes, self-help is an extremely American concept. People from medieval cultures are content to settle for their 'lot in life'..."

The truth is, in November of 2006 my view of *The Secret* was in line with my niece's, when I first began receiving forwarded emails with links to streaming video clips of the film from friends wanting to know my reaction. My preliminary response was, "Anything that takes its design cues from the Olive Garden Italian Restaurant® chain totally sucks—But wait!!! The more I look at this thing—this is the best hustle since *Borat*!"

Thankfully, I came to see that my knee jerk smugness was a defense mechanism against the scary prospect of my own personal transformation...

Keep on Sucking Till You Do Succeed

No doubt about it. Americans are success-obsessed. They're even more obsessed with success that they are with that peculiar clause about the "pursuit of happiness," so uniquely enshrined in the nation's primal manifesto.

The year *The Secret* was published was marked by a profusion of history-making celebrity meltdowns. "Stars" who had allegedly made it to the "top" self-immolated in terrifying and jaw-dropping performance pieces. This tragic odyssey is a sad cliché of what befalls so many who make it to the "big time" in America.

It could be said that "failure" is as much of a national obsession as "success." An entire genre of reality programming has been spawned where burnt-out showbiz has-beens are paid to live together in rooming houses to engage in contrived "reality." Some careers have improbably been revived: thank God there is such a thing as a Second Act in America and that this is a place where self-made billionaire Martha Stewart, having been sprung from Federal prison, can go back to her TV studio kitchen and keep showing us what "Living" is all about.

From my own perch, in one of the epicenters of American wealth and "success"—the rarified inlets of the New York beach resort area known as the Hamptons—I look around and can only conclude that "success" is very often the flipside of "self-loathing."

The homes, the Maseratis, the lip implants and $100 T-shirts are all an attempt to form an impenetrable fortress, protecting each "success story" from the reality of who he or she is. Self-loathing, whether denied, inverted or displaced, oozes from every pore of this populace. They're just normal Americans, really: Terrified human beings who never felt that they were "good enough."

In short, for all of our relative creature comforts, achieving sanity and health are an uphill battle in our particular civilization and "success" has become an increasingly confusing concept. Clearly, new definitions of what constitutes "success" are in order. I urge readers of this book to turn away from their TV sets and flashy magazines for answers and to invent your own definitions of success for YOU.

The seminars and books of the teachers featured in *The Secret*, as well as those of the additional powerhouses listed in the back of this book are some great places where you can start.

The Gilded Age Reprise

The increasingly large economic gap between the super-rich and everyone else in America is more akin to the distribution of wealth in the late 19th Century era of Robber Barons than to the mid-20th Century childhoods of the buyers of *The Secret* movie/book. This is one reason why the American market was so ripe for *The Secret* in 2007.

In Daniel Gross' *New York Times* review of Robert H. Frank's new book *Falling Behind: How Rising Inequality Harms the Middle Class,* he states:

> The rise of an overclass...is indirectly affecting the quality of life of the rest of the population—and not in a good way...[the excessive wealth of some] doesn't simply make the typical American green with envy, and hence unhappy. Rather, Frank argues, the problem is that extreme consumption...helps shape norms for the whole society, not just [the] plutocrats.

> ...since 1979, gains have flowed disproportionately to top earners...the richest 1% have seen their share of national income rise from 8.2% in 1980 to 17.4% in 2005—even the merely rich are having to overextend themselves just to keep up. "As incomes continue to grow at the top and stagnate elsewhere, we will see even more of our national income devoted to luxury goods, the main effect of which will be to raise the bar that defines what counts as luxury."[2]

Although the overall standard of living across the board in America is allegedly higher than it has ever been, it is small wonder that in this newly-dubbed "Age of Riches," where several multi-billion-dollar fortunes have been created almost overnight, right before our eyes, that everyone would want to get a piece of the action. I have begun calling this phenomenon "toxic wealth."

When chief executives are routinely paid tens of millions of dollars a year and a hedge fund manager can collect $1 billion annually, those with a few million dollars often see their accumulated wealth as puny, a reflection of their modest status in the new Gilded Age, when hundreds of thousands of people have accumulated much vaster fortunes.[3]

Success is one thing, money is another and happiness is a third, yet these all become conflated in the American psyche and it is precisely this conflation that is perpetuated and exploited by *The Secret*. Our cultural confusion around these subjects is so deftly manipulated by some of *The Secret*'s teachers that I can only hope that it is not conscious on their part; certainly, one can hardly be surprised that there are cynics who view the entire self-help industry as a vast con.

The Nostradamus of America

As mystifying as our current cultural morass appears to our 30-second attention spans, there are those who have been predicting this scenario for 30 years—and one outstanding thinker who foresaw this reality over 150 years ago.

In Alexis de Tocqueville's *Democracy in America*, published in 1835, he wrote about the New World and its fledgling democratic order. In contrast to the aristocratic system,

America was a society where making money was the dominant ethos and where the common man enjoyed a level of dignity, that was unprecedented in the Old World. In America, hard work and money dominated the minds of all, and what he described as "crass individualism" and market capitalism had taken root to an extraordinary degree.

> In Europe, de Tocqueville claimed, nobody cared about making money. The lower classes had no hope of gaining more than minimal wealth, while the upper classes found it crass, vulgar, and unbecoming of their sort to care about something as unseemly as money; many were virtually guaranteed wealth and took it for granted.[4]

The Culture of Narcissism

An equally prescient work of genius is Christopher Lasch's 1979 book, *Culture of Narcissism*, a stunning indictment of every little thing that is so very wrong about our civilization. Some of the icky values which Lasch illuminates are those to which some of the more egregious sound bites in *The Secret* directly appeal.

In his book, Lasch set out to investigate why the most common neuroses defined by Freud in the 19th Century had morphed into totally different ones in the 20th Century United States.

Why had the legendary phobias and "nervous ailments" resulting from "repressed sexual energy" been replaced by cases of vague dissatisfactions with life and violent oscillations of self-esteem? The questions Lasch posed were essentially about the nature of the society that had produced narcissism as the dominant type of borderline personality.

> It is a society in which hierarchical relationships [are] expressed in symbols of material wealth and hedonistic life style (which after all suggests the existence of means to support such a life style)...

> [The] relationship to others is determined by the competition for obtaining these symbols: inter-personal relationships become means of this...society becomes a tool for both promoting co-operation and merciless competition...every human activity is subordinated to achieving the symbols of material wealth...

> As a result, in this society every real community (e.g. family, profession) is undermined or destroyed—the individual is completely atomized. Instead of real communities, artificial, invented communities are created that attempt, without success, to recreate the transparent and predictable social relationships that have gone with the communities on which they flourished. Finally, there is no past (as continuity with history has gone) and no future (because of uncertainty) in this society.[5]

Lasch would have us believe that Americans are in a hedonistic pissing contest and whoever dies with the most toys wins—and he's probably half-right.

Lasch certainly did not spare his criticism of the self-help movement, either. He argued that instead of liberating the personality or helping the individual to understand the world and society around him or her, the self-awareness movement served to reinforce the individual's anxiety and the de-personalization of social relationships. In his own words:

> The importance of such programs, however, lies not so much in their objectives as in the anxiety to which they appeal and the vision of reality that informs them—the perception that success depends on psychological manipulation and that all of life, even the ostensibly achievement-oriented realm of work, centers on the struggle for interpersonal advantage, the deadly game of intimidating friends and seducing people.[6]

As much of a fan as I am of the passion and the truth in Lasch's stygian rant, his views are overly dark and offer absolutely no solutions for this hellacious psychological landscape.

I say, as do the speakers in *The Secret*, that we CAN choose our value systems and it can start with something as small as a shift from feelings of lack for what one does

NOT have to feelings of gratitude for what one DOES have. This is a rapid and almost magical experience—although the truth is that it's a result of a series of chemical reactions in the brain. That momentary "magic" needs to be sustained by a set of practices, be they spiritual, physical—or ideally both, that will support the happy brain/body/spirit state. The more seasoned self-help professionals will tell you it can take a lot of work, years, even to re-program yourself. But if you're sick of getting the same results, it is probably worth it to change your routines.

An interesting thing about the Chinese approach to medicine and health is one of constantly taking steps to support your "Chi" or lifeforce. It's not about prevention of illness, it's about always choosing what is good for you. You see millions of people in China waking up well before work every morning to congregate in the public squares to do Tai Chi exercises. In many ways, health is embedded in Chinese culture, in a way that it is not in the West.

So, What Happened to Happiness?

Whatever did become of the "pursuit of happiness"? Author Darrin McMahon made himself the world's expert on the subject, in his book *Happiness: A History*,[7] which charts the evolution of this elusive state, the pursuit of which is primordially enshrined in legalese for all Americans...indeed, happiness has come to be perceived as practically a duty.

Through McMahon's study of ideals of happiness in Western culture, from the ancient Greeks to the present, we find that this was hardly the norm.

> It is "one of the delicious ironies of history" that "Marx's contention that not only should we enjoy the fruits of our labor, but labor itself should be our fruit, is today a central tenet of the capitalist creed."[8]

In short, happiness is a creation, its very labile and it's ultimately a choice that is up to each and every one of us to make—or to decline.

The Bardo

Tibetan Buddhists use the word *bardo* to describe transitional states that lie between two other states, such as the "bardo of dream," which lies between waking consciousness and the dream state and the "bardo of dying,"[9] between life and death. Terrifying hallucinations are a common feature of *bardos*, which essentially represent the fears of the percipient.

For many viewers, I think that *The Secret* represents a kind of *bardo* or gateway between life as they know it and life as it could be. I think that much of the criticism that

I and others have so eagerly unleashed upon *The Secret* is the result of how confronting and threatening the teachings of this film can be to our self-image and to our feelings about the choices we have made in our lives.

People will sabotage the *The Secret*'s message, its messengers (and themselves) until they are at peace with the knowledge that it is a matter of their own personal choice, whether they wish to clarify for themselves what they truly want out of life, take all the actions necessary to achieve their goals and how they will choose to respond to circumstances along the way.

Selling the American Dream Back to the Americans

As a neophyte in the worlds of spiritual development and self-help, Rhonda has made some notable gaffes but I've actually come to view Rhonda's greenness as cute, when I realize just how recently she came upon American New Thought and self-help ideas and how quickly she managed to inspire her Australian production team to create this movie, based on ideas that were not particularly in favor Down Under.

Rhonda is the first to admit that she is a newcomer to the world of New Thought and self-improvement, touting her relative lack of experience in this field as a plus: "Sometimes, less information is better!"[10] It is unquestionable that her fresh excitement about the half-forgotten ideals of New Thought and her dogged application and success in their deployment has re-energized the businesses of countless motivational speakers, bringing highly-effective self-help to a broader global audience than ever before.

This team dared to dream that they could generate local excitement but instead came up against the endemic British-style cultural resistance to that "loathsome self-help crap." It was in America that they ultimately found outrageous success, selling the American Dream back to the Americans.

The likely answer to the question of why *The Secret* caught fire in America is that after five years of war fatigue and execrable political leadership, Americans wanted their Dream back.

No Excuses

The mass marketing of complex metaphysical concepts can lead to a distorted message, despite the best efforts of those who communicate it and especially if their understanding of them isn't very deep. I share the concern of others that many of Rhonda's pronouncements are tainted with the same kind of superficial, misleading, magical thinking that has dogged the New Age movement since its beginnings.

However, I will not let any untoward flakiness stop me from being inspired by the empowering things that she and the other teachers have to say. I will not let anybody's past sketchiness stop me from becoming more grateful for what I have access to and from improving my overall disposition. I will not let my disappointment over certain shallow statements made by some of the teachers stop me from becoming present to how I, myself have not always made brilliant statements or choices and how I can choose to see things differently and speak of them in a more powerful light. I will not let my having different values from some of the teachers stop me from taking their good ideas to put into practice and make my life more enjoyable.

Whether or not one believes in a linear afterlife in Heaven or Hell or reincarnated in another body—or occurring simultaneously in an infinitude of parallel universes—excess suffering doesn't seem necessary, unless you go in for that sort of thing!

There are any number of excuses for people not to avail themselves of what is being offered by *The Secret*, especially when these excuses further their unconscious self-sabotage. It's up to each individual whether or not they're going to allow the doltish statements of others or cheesy graphics or somebody's hairdo to get in the way of their own self-empowerment. What excuse are you going to use to stop you from having a life you love, without any reservation?

The Secret is Right Under Your Nose

Many critics argued that there was "no secret" to *The Secret*, but having spent considerable time thinking about this, I would say that the accessibility of self-empowerment is a secret that lurks out in the open. The integrated practice of gratitude, clarity of purpose and maintaining a positive outlook can transform every life and it is free of charge to anyone who will take time to truly take care of themselves and to actually do these things.

While most people can intellectually understand the benefits of these practices, not everyone actually practices them (either due to unconscious resistance, self-sabotage or lack of information about what practices would resolve their specific needs). The full effects of these practices therefore, do remain relatively unknown or "secret" to the world at-large.

FURTHER READING/VIEWING

SELF-EMPOWERMENT BOOKS

Assaraf, John. 2007. *Having it All: Achieving Your Life's Goals and Dreams.* (Atria).

Attwood, Janet. 2007. *The Passion Test: The Effortless Path to Discovering Your Destiny.* (Hudson Street Press).

Beckwith, Michael. 2000. *40 Day Mind Fast Soul Feast.* (Agape Publishing).

Canfield, Jack. 2006. *The Success Principles™: How to Get from Where You Are to Where You Want to Be.* (Collins).

Demartini, John. 2002. *The Breakthrough Experience: A Revolutionary New Approach to Personal Transformation.* (Hay House).

Diamond, Marie. 2007. *The Very Simple Law of Attraction: Find Out What You Really Want from Life...and Get It!* (Burman Books).

Dooley, Mike. 2007. *Notes from the Universe: New Perspectives from an Old Friend.* (Atria Books)

Doyle, Bob. 2006. *Wealth Beyond Reason.* (Trafford Publishing).

Dwoskin, Hale (with Jack Canfield). 2003. *The Sedona Method: Your Key to Lasting Happiness, Success, Peace and Emotional Well-Being.* (Sedona Press).

Emery, Stewart. 2007 ed. *Success Built to Last: Creating a Life that Matters.* (Plume).

Goodman, Morris. 1985. *The Miracle Man: The Inspiring Story of the Human Spirit.* (Simon & Schuster).

Gray, John. 2004 ed. *Men Are from Mars, Women Are from Venus: The Classic Guide to Understanding the Opposite Sex.* (Harper Paperbacks).

Harris, Bill. 2002. *Thresholds of the Mind.* (Centerpointe Press).

Holmes, Chet. 2007. *The Ultimate Sales Machine: Turbocharge Your Business with Relentless Focus on 12 Key Strategies*. (Portfolio Hardcover).

Langmeier, Loral. 2005. *The Millionaire Maker: Act, Think, and Make Money the Way the Wealthy Do*. (McGraw-Hill).

Levinson, Jay Conrad. *Guerrilla Marketing, 4th ed.: Easy and Inexpensive Strategies for Making Big Profits From Your Small Business*. (Houghton Mifflin).

Nichols, Lisa. 2006. *Chicken Soup for the African American Woman's Soul*. (HCI).

Proctor, Bob. 1997. *You Were Born Rich: Now You Can Discover and Develop Those Riches*. (LifeSuccess Productions).

Ray, James Arthur. 1999. *The Science of Success: How to Attract Prosperity and Create Harmonic Wealth Through Proven Principles*. (Sun Ark Press).

Shimoff, Marci (with Carol Kline). 2008. *Happy for No Reason: 7 Steps to Being Happy from the Inside Out*. (Free Press).

Vitale, Joe (with Bob Proctor). 2001. *Spiritual Marketing: A Proven 5-Step Formula for Easily Creating Wealth from the Inside Out*. (1st Books Library).

Waitley, Denis. 1986 *The Psychology of Winning*. (Berkley).

Wilber, Ken. 2007. *The Integral Vision: A Very Short Introduction to the Revolutionary Integral Approach to Life, God, the Universe, and Everything*. (Shambhala) and 2001. *Sex, Ecology, Spirituality: The Spirit of Evolution, Second Edition*. (Shambhala).

Wolf, Fred Alan. 2005. *Dr. Quantum's Little Book Of Big Ideas: Where Science Meets Spirit*. (Moment Point Press).

RELATED WEBSITES

Abraham-Hicks Publications
http://www.abraham-hicks.com

Agape Live (Michael Beckwith's Service)
http://www.agapelive.com

Bob Proctor: LifeSuccess Productions
http://www.bobproctor.com

Bill Harris: Centerpointe Research Institute
http://www.centerpointe.com

Dr.Demartini.com
http://www.drdemartini.com

Fred Alan Wolf: "Dr. Quantum"
http://www.fredalanwolf.com

Janet Attwood: Enlightened Alliances
http://www.enlightenedalliances.com

Jay Levinson: Guerrilla Marketing
http://www.gmarketing.com

Jack Canfield: America's Success Coach
http://www.jackcanfield.com

James Arthur Ray: Balance is bogus! Only harmony yields happiness
and real wealth...
http://jamesray.com

Joe Vitale is...Mr. Fire
http://www.mrfire.com

John Assaraf: More Money. More Life. More Love.
http://www.johnassaraf.com

Ken Wilber
http://www.kenwilber.com and http://www.integralinstitute.org

Lisa Nichols: The Law of Attraction Teacher in *The Secret*
http://www.lisa-nichols.com

Loral Langemeier: We Make Millionaires
http://www.liveoutloud.com

Marci Shimoff Keynote Speaker & Author
http://www.marcishimoff.com

Marie Diamond Tips for Decorating; Feng Shui
http://www.mariediamond.com

Morris Goodman "The Miracle Man"
http://www.themiracleman.org

Official Sedona Method
http://www.sedona.com

Official Website of TUT's Adventurers Club
http://www.tut.com

Success Built to Last
http://www.successbuilttolast.com

The Chet Holmes Method
http://www.chetholmes.com

The Waitley Institute
http://www.waitley.com

Wealth Beyond Reason: The Truth About The Law of Attraction
http://www.wealthbeyondreason.com

World of John Gray
http://www.marsvenus.com

NEW THOUGHT BOOKS

Allen, James. 2005 ed. *As a Man Thinketh*. (Wildside Press).

Cady, Emilie. 2004 ed. *The Complete Works of Emilie Cady*. (Unity School of Christianity).

Eddy, Mary Baker. 1875. *Science and Health with Key to the Scriptures*. (Indypublish.com) 2002 ed.

Emerson, Ralph Waldo. 2006. *The Essays of Ralph Waldo Emerson (Collected Works of Ralph Waldo Emerson)*. (Belknap Press).

Fillmore, Charles. 2006 eds: *Prosperity* and *Atom-Smashing Power of the Mind*. (Unity Classic Library).

Fillmore, Myrtle. 2006 ed. *Healing Letters*. (Unity Classic Library).

Haanel, Charles. 2006 ed. *The Master Key System*. (Filiquarian Publishing, LLC).

Hill, Napoleon. 2004 ed. *Think and Grow Rich [Restored and Revised]*. (Aventine Press).

Hopkins, Emma Curtis. 2007 ed. *Scientific Christian Mental Practice*. (Cosimo Classics).

Jensen, Brad. 2007 ed. *Prosperity, Step-by-Step: The Secrets of the Universe*. (Booksurge Publishing).

Mann, Mildred. 1952. *How to Find your Real Self*. (Society of Fragmatic Mysticism).

Mulford, Prentice. 2007 ed. *Thoughts are Things* (bnpublishing.com) and 1902. *The White Cross Library: Your Forces and How to Use Them*. (F.J. Needham).

Peale, Norman Vincent. 1992 ed. *Norman Vincent Peale: Three Complete Books: The Power of Positive Thinking; The Positive Principle Today; Enthusiasm Makes the Difference*. (Wings).

Quimby, Phineas. 2007 ed. *The Quimby Manuscripts*. (Cosimo Classics).

Smith, Arthur Preston. 1998. *The Power of Thought to Heal: An Ontology of Personal Faith*, (Ph.D. dissertation, Claremont).

Towne, Elizabeth. 2007 ed. *Life Power and How to Use It* (Wilder Publications).

NEW THOUGHT INTERNET

New Thought Movement Homepage:
http://www.websyte.com/alan/index.htm

QUANTUM PHYSICS BOOKS

Davies, P. C. W. 1986. *The Ghost in the Atom: A Discussion of the Mysteries of Quantum Physics*. (Cambridge University Press).

Feynman, Richard. 1985. *QED: The Strange Theory of Light and Matter*. (Princeton University Press).

Greene, Brian. 2000. *The Elegant Universe: Superstrings, Hidden Dimensions, and the Quest for the Ultimate Theory*. (Vintage).

Goswami, Amit. 1995. *The Self-Aware Universe*. (Tarcher).

Hawking, Stephen. 1998. *A Brief History of Time: The Updated and Expanded Tenth Anniversary Edition*. (Bantam).

Heisenberg, Werner. 1958. *Physics and Philosophy: The Revolution in Modern Science*. (Harper and Row).

Heisenberg, Werner. 1971. *Physics and Beyond: Encounters and Conversations*. (Harper and Row).

Herbert, Nick. 1987. *Quantum Reality: Beyond the New Physics*. (Anchor Books).

Kaku, Michio. 1995. *Hyperspace: A Scientific Odyssey Through Parallel Universes, Time Warps, and the 10th Dimension*. (Anchor Books).

McFarlane, Thomas. Summer-Fall 1999. "The Illusion of Materialism: How Quantum Physics Contradicts the Belief in an Objective World Existing Independent of Observation." *Center Voice: The Newsletter of the Center for Sacred Sciences*.

Penrose, Roger. 2005. *The Road to Reality: A Complete Guide to the Laws of the Universe*. (Knopf).

Satinover, Jeffrey. 2002. *The Quantum Brain: The Search for Freedom and the Next Generation of Man*. (Wiley).

Zukav, Gary. 1990. *The Dancing Wu Li Masters*. (Bantam Books).

QUANTUM PHYSICS INTERNET

Heisenberg and Uncertainty: A Web Exhibit American Institute of Physics: www.aip.org/history/heisenberg

Measurement in Quantum Mechanics: Frequently Asked Questions edited by Paul Budnik: www.mtnmath.com/faq/meas-qm.html

The Particle Adventure: An interactive tour of fundamental particles and forces, Lawrence Berkeley National Laboratory: www.particleadventure.org

Discussions with Einstein on Epistemological Problems in Atomic Physics, Niels Bohr (1949): www.marxists.org/reference/subject/philosophy/works/dk/bohr.htm

The History of Quantum Theory, Werner Heisenberg (1958): www.marxists.org/reference/subject/philosophy/works/ge/heisenb2.htm

The Copenhagen Interpretation of Quantum Theory, Werner Heisenberg (1958): www.marxists.org/reference/subject/philosophy/works/ge/heisenb3.htm

The Illusion of Materialism by Thomas J. McFarlane: www.integralscience.org/materialism/materialism.html

Quantum Future: http://quantumfuture.net/quantum_future

MYSTICISM, THEOSOPHY & ALCHEMY BOOKS

Blavatsky, Helena Petrovna. Originally published in 1888. *The Secret Doctrine*. (Quest Books; Reissue Edition).

Cayce, Edgar Evans and Cayce, Hugh Lynn. 1988. *Edgar Cayce on Atlantis*. (Warner Books; Reissue Edition).

Churchward, James. 1988. *The Children of Mu*. (Brotherhood of Life; Reprint Edition).

Fulcanelli. 1999. *The Dwellings of the Philosophers*. (Archive Press & Communications).

Gurdjieff, G.I. 1969. *Meetings With Remarkable Men (Arkana S.)*. (Penguin Books; New Edition).

Kharitidi, Olga. 1997. *Entering the Circle: Ancient Secrets of Siberian Wisdom Discovered by a Russian Psychiatrist*. (HarperSanFrancisco).

Krishnamurti, Jiddu. 1975. *Freedom from the Known*. (HarperSanFrancisco).

Ouspensky, P.D. 2001. *In Search of the Miraculous: Fragments of an Unknown Teaching.* (Harvest/HBJ Book; New Edition).

Velikovsky, Immanuel. 1984. *Worlds in Collision.* (Pocket; Reissue Edition).

CHANNELING BOOKS

Anonymous. 1955. *The Urantia Book* (Urantia Foundation). New 2000 Hardcover ed.

Marciniak, Barbara. 1992. *Bringers of the Dawn: Teachings from the Pleiadians.* (Bear & Company).

Marciniak, Barbara. 1994. *Earth: Pleiadian Keys to the Living Library.* (Bear & Company).

Roberts, Jane. 1994. *The Nature of Personal Reality: Specific, Practical Techniques for Solving Everyday Problems and Enriching the Life You Know.* (Amber-Allen Publishing; Reprint Edition).

Roberts, Jane. 1994. *Seth Speaks: The Eternal Validity of the Soul.* (Amber-Allen Publishing; Reprint Edition).

Royal, Lyssa and Priest, Keith. 1993. *The Prism of Lyra: An Exploration of Human Galactic Heritage.* (Light Technology Publications; Revised Edition).

Shucman, Helen. 1972. *A Course in Miracles.* (Course in Miracles Society).

CHANNELING INTERNET

The Cassiopaean Experiment:
http://www.cassiopaea.com

Wikipedia: Text of the GNU Free Documentation License
Version 1.2, November 2002

PREAMBLE

The purpose of this License is to make a manual, textbook, or other functional and useful document "free" in the sense of freedom: to assure everyone the effective freedom to copy and redistribute it, with or without modifying it, either commercially or noncommercially. Secondarily, this License preserves for the author and publisher a way to get credit for their work, while not being considered responsible for modifications made by others.

This License is a kind of "copyleft", which means that derivative works of the document must themselves be free in the same sense. It complements the GNU General Public License, which is a copyleft license designed for free software.

We have designed this License in order to use it for manuals for free software, because free software needs free documentation: a free program should come with manuals providing the same freedoms that the software does. But this License is not limited to software manuals; it can be used for any textual work, regardless of subject matter or whether it is published as a printed book. We recommend this License principally for works whose purpose is instruction or reference.

APPLICABILITY AND DEFINITIONS

This License applies to any manual or other work, in any medium, that contains a notice placed by the copyright holder saying it can be distributed under the terms of this License. Such a notice grants a world-wide, royalty-free license, unlimited in duration, to use that work under the conditions stated herein. The "Document", below, refers to any such manual or work. Any member of the public is a licensee, and is addressed as "you". You accept the license if you copy, modify or distribute the work in a way requiring permission under copyright law.

A "Modified Version" of the Document means any work containing the Document or a portion of it, either copied verbatim, or with modifications and/or translated into another language.

A "Secondary Section" is a named appendix or a front-matter section of the Document that deals exclusively with the relationship of the publishers or authors of the Document to the Document's overall subject (or to related matters) and contains nothing that could fall directly within that overall subject. (Thus, if the Document is in part a textbook of mathematics, a Secondary Section may not explain any mathematics.) The relationship could be a matter of historical connection with the subject or with related matters, or of legal, commercial, philo-sophical, ethical or political position regarding them.

The "Invariant Sections" are certain Secondary Sections whose titles are designated, as being those of Invariant Sections, in the notice that says that the Document is released under this License. If a section does not fit the above definition of Secondary then it is not allowed to be designated as Invariant. The Document may contain zero Invariant Sections. If the Document does not identify any Invariant Sections then there are none.

The "Cover Texts" are certain short passages of text that are listed, as Front-Cover Texts or Back-Cover Texts, in the notice that says that the Document is released under this License. A Front-Cover Text may be at most 5 words, and a Back-Cover Text may be at most 25 words.

A "Transparent" copy of the Document means a machine-readable copy, represented in a format whose specification is available to the general public, that is suitable for revising the document straightforwardly with generic text editors or (for images composed of pixels) generic paint programs or (for drawings) some widely available drawing editor, and that is suitable for input to text formatters or for automatic translation to a variety of formats suitable for input to text formatters. A copy made in an otherwise Transparent file format whose markup, or absence of markup, has been arranged to thwart or discourage subsequent modification by readers is not Transparent. An image format is not Transparent if used for any substantial amount of text. A copy that is not "Transparent" is called "Opaque".

Examples of suitable formats for Transparent copies include plain ASCII without markup, Texinfo input format, LaTeX input format, SGML or XML using a publicly available DTD, and standard-conforming simple HTML, PostScript or PDF designed for human modification. Examples of transparent image formats include PNG, XCF and JPG. Opaque formats include proprietary formats that can be read and edited only by proprietary word processors, SGML or XML for which the DTD and/or processing tools are not generally available, and the machine-generated HTML, PostScript or PDF produced by some word processors for output purposes only.

The "Title Page" means, for a printed book, the title page itself, plus such following pages as are needed to hold, legibly, the material this License requires to appear in the title page. For works in formats which do not have any title page as such, "Title Page" means the text near the most prominent appearance of the work's title, preceding the beginning of the body of the text.

A section "Entitled XYZ" means a named subunit of the Document whose title either is precisely XYZ or contains XYZ in parentheses following text that translates XYZ in another language. (Here XYZ stands for a specific section name mentioned below, such as "Acknowledgements", "Dedications", "Endorsements", or "History".) To "Preserve the Title" of such a section when you modify the Document means that it remains a section "Entitled XYZ" according to this definition.

The Document may include Warranty Disclaimers next to the notice which states that this License applies to the Document. These Warranty Disclaimers are considered to be included by reference in this License, but only as regards disclaiming warranties: any other implication that these Warranty Disclaimers may have is void and has no effect on the meaning of this License.

VERBATIM COPYING

You may copy and distribute the Document in any medium, either commercially or noncommercially, provided that this License, the copyright notices, and the license notice saying this License applies to the Document are reproduced in all copies, and that you add no other conditions whatsoever to those of this License. You may not use technical measures to obstruct or control the reading or further copying of the copies you make or distribute. However, you may accept compensation in exchange for copies. If you distribute a large enough number of copies you must also follow the conditions in section 3.

You may also lend copies, under the same conditions stated above, and you may publicly display copies.

COPYING IN QUANTITY

If you publish printed copies (or copies in media that commonly have printed covers) of the Document, numbering more than 100, and the Document's license notice requires Cover Texts, you must enclose the copies in covers that carry, clearly and legibly, all these Cover Texts: Front-Cover Texts on the front cover, and Back-Cover Texts on the back cover. Both covers must also clearly and legibly identify you as the publisher of these copies. The front cover must present the full title with all words of the title equally prominent and visible. You may add other material on the covers in addition. Copying with changes limited to the covers, as long as they preserve the title of the Document and satisfy these conditions, can be treated as verbatim copying in other respects.

If the required texts for either cover are too voluminous to fit legibly, you should put the first ones listed (as many as fit reasonably) on the actual cover, and continue the rest onto adjacent pages.

If you publish or distribute Opaque copies of the Document numbering more than 100, you must either include a machine-readable Transparent copy along with each Opaque copy, or state in or with each Opaque copy a computer-network location from which the general network-using public has access to download using public-standard network protocols a complete Transparent copy of the Document, free of added material. If you use the latter option, you must take reasonably prudent steps, when you begin distribution of Opaque copies in quantity, to ensure that this Transparent copy will remain thus accessible at the stated location until at least one year after the last time you distribute an Opaque copy (directly or through your agents or retailers) of that edition to the public.

It is requested, but not required, that you contact the authors of the Document well before redistributing any large number of copies, to give them a chance to provide you with an updated version of the Document.

MODIFICATIONS

You may copy and distribute a Modified Version of the Document under the conditions of sections 2 and 3 above, provided that you release the Modified Version under precisely this License, with the Modified Version filling the role of the Document, thus licensing distribution and modification of the Modified Version to whoever possesses a copy of it. In addition, you must do these things in the Modified Version:

A. Use in the Title Page (and on the covers, if any) a title distinct from that of the Document, and from those of previous versions (which should, if there were any, be listed in the History section of the Document). You may use the same title as a previous version if the original publisher of that version gives permission.

B. List on the Title Page, as authors, one or more persons or entities responsible for authorship of the modifications in the Modified Version, together with at least five of the principal authors of the Document (all of its principal authors, if it has fewer than five), unless they release you from this requirement.

C. State on the Title page the name of the publisher of the Modified Version, as the publisher.

D. Preserve all the copyright notices of the Document.

E. Add an appropriate copyright notice for your modifications adjacent to the other copyright notices.

F. Include, immediately after the copyright notices, a license notice giving the public permission to use the Modified Version under the terms of this License, in the form shown in the Addendum below.

G. Preserve in that license notice the full lists of Invariant Sections and required Cover Texts given in the Document's license notice.

H. Include an unaltered copy of this License.

I. Preserve the section Entitled "History", Preserve its Title, and add to it an item stating at least the title, year, new authors, and publisher of the Modified Version as given on the Title Page. If there is no section Entitled "History" in the Document, create one stating the title, year, authors, and publisher of the Document as given on its Title Page, then add an item describing the Modified Version as stated in the previous sentence.

J. Preserve the network location, if any, given in the Document for public access to a Transparent copy of the Document, and likewise the network locations given in the Document for previous versions it was based on. These may be placed in the "History" section. You may omit a network location for a work that was published at least four years before the Document itself, or if the original publisher of the version it refers to gives permission.

K. For any section Entitled "Acknowledgements" or "Dedications", Preserve the Title of the section, and preserve in the section all the substance and tone of each of the contributor acknowledgements and/or dedications given therein.

L. Preserve all the Invariant Sections of the Document, unaltered in their text and in their titles. Section numbers or the equivalent are not considered part of the section titles.

M. Delete any section Entitled "Endorsements". Such a section may not be included in the Modified Version.

N. Do not retitle any existing section to be Entitled "Endorsements" or to conflict in title with any Invariant Section.

O. Preserve any Warranty Disclaimers.

If the Modified Version includes new front-matter sections or appendices that qualify as Secondary Sections and contain no material copied from the Document, you may at your option designate some or all of these sections as invariant. To do this, add their titles to the list of Invariant Sections in the Modified Version's license notice. These titles must be distinct from any other section titles.

You may add a section Entitled "Endorsements", provided it contains nothing but endorsements of your Modified Version by various parties—for example, statements of peer review or that the text has been approved by an organization as the authoritative definition of a standard.

You may add a passage of up to five words as a Front-Cover Text, and a passage of up to 25 words as a Back-Cover Text, to the end of the list of Cover Texts in the Modified Version. Only one passage of Front-Cover Text and one of Back-Cover Text may be added by (or through arrangements made by) any one entity. If the Document already includes a cover text for the same cover, previously added by you or by arrangement made by the same entity you are acting on behalf of, you may not add another; but you may replace the old one, on explicit permission from the previous publisher that added the old one.

The author(s) and publisher(s) of the Document do not by this License give permission to use their names for publicity for or to assert or imply endorsement of any Modified Version.

COMBINING DOCUMENTS

You may combine the Document with other documents released under this License, under the terms defined in section 4 above for modified versions, provided that you include in the combination all of the Invariant Sections of all of the original documents, unmodified, and list them all as Invariant Sections of your combined work in its license notice, and that you preserve all their Warranty Disclaimers.

The combined work need only contain one copy of this License, and multiple identical Invariant Sections may be replaced with a single copy. If there are multiple Invariant Sections with the same name but different contents, make the title of each such section unique by adding at the end of it, in parentheses, the name of the original author or publisher of that section if known, or else a unique number. Make the same adjustment to the section titles in the list of Invariant Sections in the license notice of the combined work.

In the combination, you must combine any sections Entitled "History" in the various original documents, forming one section Entitled "History"; likewise combine any sections Entitled "Acknowledgements", and any sections Entitled "Dedications". You must delete all sections Entitled "Endorsements."

COLLECTIONS OF DOCUMENTS

You may make a collection consisting of the Document and other documents released under this License, and replace the individual copies of this License in the various documents with a single copy that is included in the collection, provided that you follow the rules of this License for verbatim copying of each of the documents in all other respects.

You may extract a single document from such a collection, and distribute it individually under this License, provided you insert a copy of this License into the extracted document, and follow this License in all other respects regarding verbatim copying of that document.

AGGREGATION WITH INDEPENDENT WORKS

A compilation of the Document or its derivatives with other separate and independent documents or works, in or on a volume of a storage or distribution medium, is called an "aggregate" if the copyright resulting from the compilation is not used to limit the legal rights of the compilation's users beyond what the individual works permit. When the Document is included in an aggregate, this License does not apply to the other works in the aggregate which are not themselves derivative works of the Document.

If the Cover Text requirement of section 3 is applicable to these copies of the Document, then if the Document is less than one half of the entire aggregate, the Document's Cover Texts may be placed on covers that bracket the Document within the aggregate, or the electronic equivalent of covers if the Document is in electronic form. Otherwise they must appear on printed covers that bracket the whole aggregate.

TRANSLATION

Translation is considered a kind of modification, so you may distribute translations of the Document under the terms of section 4. Replacing Invariant Sections with translations requires special permission from their copyright holders, but you may include translations of some or all Invariant Sections in addition to the original versions of these Invariant Sections. You may include a translation of this License, and all the license notices in the Document, and any Warranty Disclaimers, provided that you also include the original English version of this License and the original versions of those notices and disclaimers. In case of a disagreement between the translation and the original version of this License or a notice or disclaimer, the original version will prevail.

If a section in the Document is Entitled "Acknowledgements", "Dedications", or "History", the requirement (section 4) to Preserve its Title (section 1) will typically require changing the actual title.

TERMINATION

You may not copy, modify, sublicense, or distribute the Document except as expressly provided for under this License. Any other attempt to copy, modify, sublicense or distribute the Document is void, and will automatically terminate your rights under this License. However, parties who have received copies, or rights, from you under this License will not have their licenses terminated so long as such parties remain in full compliance.

FUTURE REVISIONS OF THIS LICENSE

The Free Software Foundation may publish new, revised versions of the GNU Free Documentation License from time to time. Such new versions will be similar in spirit to the present version, but may differ in detail to address new problems or concerns. See http://www.gnu.org/copyleft.

Each version of the License is given a distinguishing version number. If the Document specifies that a particular numbered version of this License "or any later version" applies to it, you have the option of following the terms and conditions either of that specified version or of any later version that has been published (not as a draft) by the Free Software Foundation. If the Document does not specify a version number of this License, you may choose any version ever published (not as a draft) by the Free Software Foundation.

ENDNOTES

CHAPTER 1—THE BUSINESS END OF *THE SECRET*

[1] http://thesecret.tv/behind-the-secret-making-of.html.

[2] Canfield, J. May 2007, "The Time 100 People Who Shape Our World," *Time*.

[3] For some perspective on *What The Bleep Do We Know?!* see my 2005 book, *Beyond The Bleep*.

[4] Ressner, J. December 28, 2006, "The Secret of Success," *Time*.

[5] http://www.emeraldforest.com/vividaswhitepaper.pdf.

[6] Memmott, C. February 14, 2007, "'Secret' attracts plenty of attention," *USA TODAY*.

[7] Steinmetz, M. April 2007, "'The Secret' is Out (of Stock)," *Book Business*.

[8] Salkin, A. February 25, 2007, "Shaking Riches Out of the Cosmos," *New York Times* Section 9, Page 1.

[9] Ibid.

[10] Jerry & Esther's Statement on "The Secret" http://abrahamhicks.meetup.com/70/boards/view/viewthread?thread=2283719.

CHAPTER 2—THE NEW THOUGHT MOVEMENT

[1] Adler, J. March 5, 2007, "Decoding 'The Secret,'" *Newsweek*.

[2] Wattles, W. 1910, *The Science of Getting Rich*.

[3] Melanson, T. April 11, 2007, *Oprah Winfrey, New Thought, "The Secret" and the "New Alchemy,"* conspiracyarchive.com (Redacted and edited with permission from Terry Melanson).

[4] http://www.thesecret.tv/pastteachers.html.

[5] Isaac Newton's translation of the Emerald Tablet: http://en.wikipedia.org/wiki/Emerald_Tablet.

[6] http://prenticemulford.wwwhubs.com.

[7] The College of Divine Metaphysics: http://www.divinemetaphysics.org/Metaphysics.html.

[8] http://charleshaanel.wwwhubs.com.

[9] Agape website: http://www.agapelive.com.

[10] Unity Church of Fort Worth, TX website: http://www.unityfortworth.org/leadership.html.

CHAPTER 3—ABRAHAM & THE LAW OF ATTRACTION

[1] Abraham MP3: http://www.abraham-hicks.com/MP3downloads.php.

[2] Abraham Teachings: http://www.abraham-hicks.com.

[3] Redacted transcript of video posted on YouTube: http://www.youtube.com/profile?user=AbrahamHicks.

[4] Hicks, E. and J. 2007. *The Astonishing Power of Emotions* (Hay House).

[5] Bruce, A. 2005. *Beyond the Bleep: The Unauthorized Guide to What the Bleep Do We Know!?* (The Disinformation Company).

[6] Salkin, A. February 25, 2007, "Shaking Riches Out of the Cosmos," *New York Times* Section 9, Page 1.

CHAPTER 4—THE *CHICKEN SOUP* POSSE

[1] Hughes, D. "An Interview with Jack Canfield, Co-Author of *Chicken Soup for the Soul*®." Share Guide Holistic Health Magazine & Resource

Directory: http://www.shareguide.com/Canfield3.html.

[2] © Jack Canfield. Adapted from *The Success Principles: How to Get from Where You Are to Where You Want to Be* by Jack Canfield with Janet Switzer (HarperResource, 2005; ISBN: 0-06-059488-8). Jack Canfield, America's Success Coach, is the founder and co-creator of the billion-dollar book brand *Chicken Soup For The Soul*® and the nation's leading authority on Peak Performance. If you're ready to jump-start your life, make more money, and have more fun and joy in all that you do, get your *free* success tips from Jack Canfield now at http://www.JackCanfield.com.

[3] Chicken Soup for African-American Soul:
http://www.africanamericansoul.com/african-american-womans-soul.htm.

[4] CNN Transcripts, March 8, 2007, http://transcripts.cnn.com/TRANSCRIPTS/0703/08/lkl.01.html.

[5] Lisa Nichols Motivating the Teen Spirit:
http://www.lisa-nichols.com/lisa_nichols/speaking_topics.htm.

[6] *Jamaica Observer*, August 13, 2006
http://www.jamaicaobserver.com/lifestyle/html/20060812t210000-0500_111117_obs_warm____hearty_.asp

[7] http://www.lisa-nichols.com/oprah/specialreport.pdf.

[8] Marci Shimoff *Happy for No Reason*:
http://www.marcishimoff.com/happyfornoreason.html.

CHAPTER 5—*THE SECRET* WEALTH COACHES

[1] http://lighthousecoaching.thesgrprogram.com.

[2] Create Success Seminars:
http://www.horncreek.com/bobproctor.html.

[3] Cheesy Money-Grab:
http://lighthousecoaching.thesgrprogram.com.

[4] http://www.empoweredwealth.com/new_logo.html

[5] A Conversation with Loral Langemeier at http://www.audiomotivation.com.

[6] Langmeier's site: http://www.liveoutloud.com/ aboutpurposeandvalues.php.

[7] Op. Cit. http://www.liveoutloud.com/pressreleases/050707.php.

[8] A Conversation with Loral Langemeier at: http://www.audiomotivation.com.

[9] John Assaraf's website: http://www.onecoach.com/Public/ AboutUs/index.cfm

[10] http://thephantomwriters.com/free_content/d/a/key-2-outstanding-results.shtml.

[11] http://www.tradingedge.com.au/About_david.asp.

[12] Ibid.

[13] Martin, G. & Puthenpurackal, J. "Imitation is the Sincerest Form of Flattery: Warren Buffett and Berkshire Hathaway," Available at: http://www.fma.org/Chicago/Papers/Imitation_Is_the_ Sincerest_Form_of_Flattery.pdf.

[14] Buffett is often referred to as "the oracle of Omaha" due to his long-time residence in Omaha, Nebraska.

[15] David Schirmer's May 24, 2007 post on The Secret Forum: http://thesecret.powerfulintentions.com/forum/thesecret/ message-view/17289062.

[16] http://www.youtube.com/watch?v=CM1tGHOkgdA&mode= related&search=.

[17] http://www.youtube.com/watch?v=C-hG8y-Jnuc.

CHAPTER 6—MIND TECHNOLOGY

[1] Make a Change Personal Discovery Journeys: http://www.makeachangejourneys.com.

[2] Bill Harris' website: http://www.centerpointe.com/centerpointe/?gclid=CN3Y_I2yl44CFRHzPgodik0FXA

[3] Ibid.

[4] Haines, D., 2007, 7th Edition, *Neuroanatomy: An Atlas of Structures, Sections, and Systems*, (Lippincott Williams & Wilkins).

[5] For more on Hemi-Sync® visit the Monroe Institute website at: http://www.monroeinstitute.com.

[6] http://www.buzzle.com/editorials/8-9-2005-74548.asp.

[7] The Masters of The Secret with Bill Harris http://www.themastersofthesecret.com.

[8] Dwoskin, H. 2003. *The Sedona Method: Your Key to Lasting Happiness, Success, Peace and Emotional Well-being.* p. 6.

[9] Op. Cit. p. 14.

[10] http://www.sedona.com/html/about-us-and-sedona-method.aspx.

[11] http://www.sedona.com/html/Scientific-Evidence.aspx.

[12] http://sedona.com/html/Endorsements.aspx.

[13] http://www.waitley.com/Catalog.cfm.

[14] Reproduced with permission from Denis Waitley's Weekly Ezine. To subscribe to Denis Waitley's Weekly Ezine, go to www.deniswaitley.com or send an email with Join in the subject to subscribe@deniswaitley.com. Copyright © 2005 Denis Waitley International. All rights reserved worldwide. http://www.waitley.com/Three%20Rules%20for%20Turning%20Stress%20Into%20Success.pdf.

CHAPTER 7—*THE SECRET* SCIENCE

[1] Byrne, R. 2006, *The Secret*, (Atria Books/Beyond Words), p. 156.

[2] Wolf, F.A. 2004. *The Yoga of Time Travel: How the Mind Can Defeat Time* (Quest Books) p. 116.

[3] Op. Cit. p. 13–14.

[4] Op. Cit. p. 197.

[5] Op. Cit. p. 209.

[6] Hagelin's personal website: http://hagelin.org.

[7] Occhiogrosso, P. 1996. *The Joy of Sects: A Spirited Guide to the World's Religious Traditions*. (Doubleday), p. 66.

[8] Gunzberger, R. November 4, 2000, "Presidency 2000: John S. Hagelin of Iowa: Natural Law Party Nominee," http://www.politics1.com/nlp2k.htm.

[9] Pueschel, M. July 2000, "Vedic Medicine, Meditation Receive Federal Funds," http://www.usmedicine.com.

[10] http://www.drdemartini.com/pages/about.html.

[11] http://www.drdemartini.com/pages/breakthrough.html.

[12] http://www.drdemartini.com/newsletter/December_Newsletter_Questionare.htm.

[13] http://www.drdemartini.com/pages/about.html.

[14] Adler, J. March 5, 2007, "Decoding 'The Secret,'" *Newsweek*.

[15] Fred Alan Wolf website: http://www.fredalanwolf.com/page5.htm.

[16] Wolf, F.A. 2004. *The Yoga of Time Travel: How the Mind Can Defeat Time*. (Quest Books) pp. 154–156.

[17] *What The Bleep* Newsletter: May 13, 2005. *The Bleeping Herald* Vol. 1, No. 1. http://www.whatthebleep.com/herald/issue1-quandaries.shtml.

CHAPTER 8—THE MAGIC OF *THE SECRET*

[1] Institute of Balanced and Integrated Spirituality: http://www.ibis.org.

[2] James Ray's website: http://jamesray.com/about-james-ray.php.

[3] Keynote Speakers, Inc. http://keynotespeakers.com/speaker_detail.asp?id=1046.

[4] James Ray's website: http://jamesray.com/about-james-ray.php.

[5] Institute of Balanced and Integrated Spirituality: http://ibis.org/v1/modern-magick.php.

[6] Free Republic Chatboard: http://209.157.64.200/focus/f-religion/1787493/posts.

[7] Op. Cit. 02/19/2007 7:53:59 PM PST by Gal.5:1 (emphasis by the author of this book).

[8] Institute of Balanced and Integrated Spirituality: http://www.ibis.org.

[9] Ibid.

[10] Law of Attraction Secrets: http://lawofattractionsecrets.com/blog/category hooponopono.

[11] Mike Dooley's Website: http://www.tut.com/mike_dooley_bio.htm.

[12] Mike Dooley's Website: http://www.tut.com/nftu.htm.

[13] Clayton, E. December 2002, "Interview of Mike Dooley," *Weight Watchers Magazine* (Australia).

[14] Mike Dooley's Website:
http://www.tut.com/mike_dooley_bio.htm.

[15] Clayton, E. December 2002, "Interview of Mike Dooley," *Weight Watchers Magazine* (Australia).

[16] Marie Diamond's Website:
http://info.mariediamond.com/intro_inner.htm.

[17] Marie Diamond's Website:
http://info.mariediamond.com/intro_diamond.htm.

CHAPTER 9—CHRISTIANITY & *THE SECRET*

[1] Anderson, K. 2007 "The False Teaching of 'The Secret,'" Probe.org.

[2] CNN Transcripts, March 8, 2007, http://transcripts.cnn.com/TRANSCRIPTS/0703/08/lkl.01.html.

[3] Wise, R. 2007, "The Secret: Creating One's Reality," Probe.org.

[4] http://en.wikipedia.org/wiki/Unity_Church.

[5] Neale Donald Walsch website:
http://www.nealedonaldwalsch.com/aboutneale.cfm.

[6] http://www.shareguide.com/Walsch.html.

[7] Some of the preceding and following paragraphs have been adapted from material published on the Wikipedia website. (See GNU license at back of book). http://en.wikipedia.org/wiki/Neale_Donald_Walsch

[8] Hay, V. "Neale Donald Walsch: author of bestselling *Conversations with God,* Exclusive Interview," intouchmag.com.

[9] Indigo children is a term used within the New Age movement to refer to children who allegedly represent a new evolution of the human race, possessing paranormal attributes, such as the ability to read minds.

The Indigo child concept was first publicized in 1999 by the book *The Indigo Children: The New Kids Have Arrived*, written by the husband-and-wife team of Lee Carroll and Jan Tober. Carroll insists that the concept was obtained via conversations with a spiritual entity known as Kryon.

The reason for the use of the adjective "indigo" is not universally agreed upon: some sources link it with an early researcher into the phenomenon, who was synesthetic. It has also been claimed that these children appear with an indigo-hued aura.

Adapted from Wikipedia: http://en.wikipedia.org/wiki/Indigo_children. (See GNU license at back of book).

[10] Wise, R. 1995, "Unity School of Christianity." World Religions Index, http://wri.leaderu.com.

[11] Wise, R. 2007, "The Secret: Creating One's Reality," Probe.org.

[12] The Association for Global New Thought website: http://www.agnt.org.

[13] Bruce, A. *Beyond the Bleep* (The Disinformation Company).

[14] *Prayer of Jabez* website: http://www.prayerofjabez.com/BreakthroughPages/JabezPage.html.

[15] Wilkinson, B. 2000, *The Prayer of Jabez: Breaking Through to the Blessed Life* (Multnomah) pp. 15–16.

[16] Mulholland, J. November 2001, *Religion & Ethics Newsweekly* http://www.pbs.org/wnet/religionandethics/week509/feature.html.

CHAPTER 10—THE LAW OF ATTRACTION DEBATE

[1] http://www.wealthbeyondreason.com/mystory.html.

[2] Doyle, B. 2006, *Wealth Beyond Reason*, (Trafford Publishing).

[3] http://www.holistichealthtools.com/growrich.html.

[4] Bloom, W. June 2007, "Does Everyone Really Create Their Own Reality?" http://www.williambloom.com.

[5] This is a redacted transcript that I made of Doyle's video, posted here: http://www.wealthbeyondreason.com/bobresponds.html.

[6] Op. Cit.

[7] Bruce, A. *Beyond the Bleep: The Definitive Unauthorized Guide to What the Bleep Do We Know!?*, (The Disinformation Company) p. 202.

[8] Satinover, J. 2001. *The Quantum Brain*. (Wiley & Sons) p. 217 (Emphasis added by me).

[9] http://en.wikipedia.org/wiki/Niels_Bohr.

CHAPTER 11—INTERVIEW WITH BILL HARRIS

[1] Wilber, K. 2000 *One Taste,* p. 104 Rev. 2nd ed. (Shambhala).

[2] Norcross, J. quoted by Adler, J. March 5, 2007, "Decoding 'The Secret,'" *Newsweek.*

[3] Wilber, K. 2001, *Sex, Ecology, Spirituality: The Spirit of Evolution* 2nd ed. (Shambhala).

[4] Wilber, K. 2007, *The Integral Vision: A Very Short Introduction to the Revolutionary Integral Approach to Life, God, the Universe, and Everything.* (Author comment: It's totally amazing! Buy it!).

[5] Abraham Teachings http://www.abraham-hicks.com/teachings.php.

CHAPTER 12—INTEGRALISM & THE TRICKY BUSINESS OF CREATING YOUR OWN REALITY

[1] Walker, J. & Wilber, K. "Exploring 'The Secret.' Part 1. The Tricky Business of Creating Your Own Reality." *Integral Naked* magazine, http://in.integralinstitute.org/talk.aspx?id=858 (Emphases by webmaster, not this author).

CONCLUSION—WHY *THE SECRET* HAS BEEN SO SUCCESSFUL

[1] Gross, D. August 5, 2007. "Thy Neighbor's Stash," *New York Times*.

[2] Rivlin. G., August 5, 2007, "In Silicon Valley, Millionaires Who Don't Feel Rich," *New York Times*.

[3] http://en.wikipedia.org/wiki/Alexis_de_Tocqueville.

[4] James, D. Book review of *The Culture of Narcissism: American Life in an Age of Diminishing Expectations* on the website of the CTPDC Counseling Training Centre of Liverpool, UK.

[5] Lasch, C. May 1991, *The Culture of Narcissism: American Life in an Age of Diminishing Expectations* (W. W. Norton & Company), Rev. ed. p. 66.

[6] McMahon, D. 2005, *Happiness: A History* (Atlantic Monthly Press).

[7] Nimue Ackerman, F. 2006, "Ode to Joy," *Washington Post*.

[8] Fremantle, F. 2001, *Luminous Emptiness: Understanding the Tibetan Book of the Dead*, (Shambhala), pp. 62–64.

[9] Byrne, R. 2006, *The Secret*, (Atria Books/Beyond Words), p. 135.

The Science of Getting Rich

Wallace D. Wattles

THE SCIENCE OF GETTING RICH

THE SCIENCE OF GETTING RICH

Preface

THIS book is pragmatical, not philosophical; a practical manual, not a treatise upon theories. It is intended for the men and women whose most pressing need is for money; who wish to get rich first, and philosophize afterward. It is for those who have, so far, found neither the time, the means, nor the opportunity to go deeply into the study of metaphysics, but who want results and who are willing to take the conclusions of science as a basis for action, without going into all the processes by which those conclusions were reached.

It is expected that the reader will take the fundamental statements upon faith, just as he would take statements concerning a law of electrical action if they were promulgated by a Marconi or an Edison; and, taking the statements upon faith, that he will prove their truth by acting upon them without fear or hesitation. Every man or woman who does this will certainly get rich; for the science herein applied is an exact science, and failure is impossible. For the benefit, however, of those who wish to investigate philosophical theories and so secure a logical basis for faith, I will here cite certain authorities.

The monistic theory of the universe—the theory that One is All, and that All is One; That one Substance manifests itself as the seeming many elements of the material world—is of Hindu origin, and has been gradually winning its way into the thought of the western world for two hundred years. It is the foundation of all the Oriental philosophies, and of those of Descartes, Spinoza, Leibnitz, Schopenhauer, Hegel, and Emerson.

The reader who would dig to the philosophical foundations of this is advised to read Hegel and Emerson for himself.

In writing this book I have sacrificed all other considerations to plainness and simplicity of style, so that all might understand. The plan of action laid down herein was deduced from the conclusions of philosophy; it has been thoroughly tested, and bears the supreme test of practical experiment; it works. If you wish to know how the conclusions were arrived at, read the writings of the authors mentioned above; and if you wish to reap the fruits of their philosophies in actual practice, read this book and do exactly as it tells you to do.

The Author

THE SCIENCE OF GETTING RICH

CHAPTER 1

The Right To Be Rich

WHATEVER may be said in praise of poverty, the fact remains that it is not possible to live a really complete or successful life unless one is rich. No man can rise to his greatest possible height in talent or soul development unless he has plenty of money; for to unfold the soul and to develop talent he must have many things to use, and he cannot have these things unless he has money to buy them with.

A man develops in mind, soul, and body by making use of things, and society is so organized that man must have money in order to become the possessor of things; therefore, the basis of all advancement for man must be the science of getting rich.

The object of all life is development; and everything that lives has an inalienable right to all the development it is capable of attaining.

Man's right to life means his right to have the free and unrestricted use of all the things which may be necessary to his fullest mental, spiritual, and physical unfoldment; or, in other words, his right to be rich.

In this book, I shall not speak of riches in a figurative way; to be really rich does not mean to be satisfied or contented with a little. No man ought to be satisfied with a little if he is capable of using and enjoying more. The purpose of Nature is the advancement and unfoldment of life; and every man should have all that can contribute to the power; elegance, beauty, and richness of life; to be content with less is sinful.

The man who owns all he wants for the living of all the life he is capable of living is rich; and no man who has not plenty of money can have all he wants. Life has advanced so far, and become so complex, that even the most ordinary man or woman requires a great amount of wealth in order to live in a manner that even approaches completeness. Every person naturally wants to become all that they are capable of becoming; this desire to realize innate possibilities is inherent in human nature; we cannot help wanting to be all that we can be. Success in life is becoming what you want to be; you can become what you want to be only by making use of things, and you can have the free use of things only as you become rich enough to buy them. To understand the science of getting rich is therefore the most essential of all knowledge.

There is nothing wrong in wanting to get rich. The desire for riches is really the desire for a richer, fuller, and more abundant life; and that desire is praise worthy. The man who does not desire to live more abundantly is abnormal, and so the man who does not desire to have money enough to buy all he wants is abnormal.

There are three motives for which we live; we live for the body, we live for the mind, we live for the soul. No one of these is better or holier than the other; all are alike desirable, and no one of the three—body, mind, or soul—can live fully if either of the others is cut short of full life and expression. It is not right or noble to live only for the soul and deny mind or body; and it is wrong to live for the intellect and deny body or soul.

We are all acquainted with the loathsome consequences of living for the body and denying both mind and soul; and we see that real life means the complete expression of all that man can give forth through body, mind, and soul. Whatever he can say, no man can be really happy or satisfied unless his body is living fully in every function, and unless the same is true of his mind and his soul. Wherever there is unexpressed possibility, or function not performed, there is unsatisfied desire. Desire is possibility seeking expression, or function seeking performance.

Man cannot live fully in body without good food, comfortable clothing, and warm shelter; and without freedom from excessive toil. Rest and recreation are also necessary to his physical life .

He cannot live fully in mind without books and time to study them, without opportunity for travel and observation, or without intellectual companionship.

To live fully in mind he must have intellectual recreations, and must surround himself with all the objects of art and beauty he is capable of using and appreciating.

To live fully in soul, man must have love; and love is denied expression by poverty.

A man's highest happiness is found in the bestowal of benefits on those he loves; love finds its most natural and spontaneous expression in giving. The man who has nothing to give cannot fill his place as a husband or father, as a citizen, or as a man. It is in the use of material things that a man finds full life for his body, develops his mind, and unfolds his soul. It is therefore of supreme importance to him that he should be rich.

It is perfectly right that you should desire to be rich; if you are a normal man or woman you cannot help doing so. It is perfectly right that you should give your best attention to the Science of Getting Rich, for it is the noblest and most necessary of all studies. If you neglect this study, you are derelict in your duty to yourself, to God and humanity; for you can render to God and humanity no greater service than to make the most of yourself.

CHAPTER 2

There is A Science of Getting Rich

THERE is a Science of getting rich, and it is an exact science, like algebra or arithmetic. There are certain laws which govern the process of acquiring riches; once these laws are learned and obeyed by any man, he will get rich with mathematical certainty.

The ownership of money and property comes as a result of doing things in a certain way; those who do things in this Certain Way, whether on purpose or accidentally, get rich; while those who do not do things in this Certain Way, no matter how hard they work or how able they are, remain poor.

It is a natural law that like causes always produce like effects; and, therefore, any man or woman who learns to do things in this certain way will infallibly get rich.

That the above statement is true is shown by the following facts:

Getting rich is not a matter of environment, for, if it were, all the people in certain neighborhoods would become wealthy; the people of one city would all be rich, while those of other towns would all be poor; or the inhabitants of one state would roll in wealth, while those of an adjoining state would be in poverty.

But everywhere we see rich and poor living side by side, in the same environment, and often engaged in the same vocations. When two men are in the same locality, and in the same business, and one gets rich while the other remains poor, it shows that getting rich is not, primarily, a matter of environment. Some environments may be more favorable than others, but when two men in the same business are in the same neighborhood, and one gets rich while the other fails, it indicates that getting rich is the result of doing things in a Certain Way.

And further, the ability to do things in this certain way is not due solely to the possession of talent, for many people who have great talent remain poor, while other who have very little talent get rich.

Studying the people who have got rich, we find that they are an average lot in all respects, having no greater talents and abilities than other men. It is evident that they do not get rich because they possess talents and abilities that other men have not, but because they happen to do things in a Certain Way.

Getting rich is not the result of saving, or "thrift"; many very penurious people are poor, while free spenders often get rich.

Nor is getting rich due to doing things which others fail to do; for two men in the same business often do almost exactly the same things, and one gets rich while the other remains poor or becomes bankrupt.

From all these things, we must come to the conclusion that getting rich is the result of doing things in a Certain Way.

If getting rich is the result of doing things in a Certain Way, and if like causes always produce like effects, then any man or woman who can do things in that way can become rich, and the whole matter is brought within the domain of exact science.

The question arises here, whether this Certain Way may not be so difficult that only a few may follow it. This cannot be true, as we have seen, so far as natural ability is concerned. Talented people get rich, and blockheads get rich; intellectually brilliant people get rich, and very stupid people get rich; physically strong people get rich, and weak and sickly people get rich.

Some degree of ability to think and understand is, of course, essential; but in so far natural ability is concerned, any man or woman who has sense enough to read and understand these words can certainly get rich.

Also, we have seen that it is not a matter of environment. Location counts for something; one would not go to the heart of the Sahara and expect to do successful business.

Getting rich involves the necessity of dealing with men, and of being where there are people to deal with; and if these people are inclined to deal in the way you want to deal, so much the better. But that is about as far as environment goes.

If anybody else in your town can get rich, so can you; and if anybody else in your state can get rich, so can you.

Again, it is not a matter of choosing some particular business or profession. People get rich in every business, and in every profession; while their next door neighbors in the same vocation remain in poverty.

It is true that you will do best in a business which you like, and which is congenial to you; and if you have certain talents which are well developed, you will do best in a business which calls for the exercise of those talents.

Also, you will do best in a business which is suited to your locality; an ice-cream parlor would do better in a warm climate than in Greenland, and a salmon fishery will succeed better in the Northwest than in Florida, where there are no salmon.

But, aside from these general limitations, getting rich is not dependent upon your engaging in some particular business, but upon your learning to do things in a Certain Way. If you are now in business, and anybody else in your locality is getting rich in the same business, while you are not getting rich, it is because you are not doing things in the same Way that the other person is doing them.

No one is prevented from getting rich by lack of capital. True, as you get capital the increase becomes more easy and rapid; but one who has capital is already rich, and does not need to consider how to become so. No matter how poor you may be, if you begin to do things in the Certain Way you will begin to get rich; and you will begin to have capital. The getting of capital is a part of the process of getting rich; and it is a part of the result which invariably follows the doing of things in the Certain Way. You may be the poorest man on the continent, and be deeply in debt; you may have neither friends, influence, nor resources; but if you begin to do things in this way, you must infallibly begin to get rich, for like causes must produce like effects. If you have no capital, you can get capital; if you are in the wrong business, you can get into the right business; if you are in the wrong location, you can go to the right location; and you can do so by beginning in your present business and in your present location to do things in the Certain Way which causes success.

CHAPTER 3

Is Opportunity Monopolized?

NO man is kept poor because opportunity has been taken away from him; because other people have monopolized the wealth, and have put a fence around it. You may be shut off from engaging in business in certain lines, but there are other channels open to you. Probably it would be hard for you to get control of any of the great railroad systems; that field is pretty well monopolized. But the electric railway business is still in its infancy, and offers plenty of scope for enterprise; and it will be but a very few years until traffic and transportation through the air will become a great industry, and in all its branches will give employment to hundreds of thousands, and perhaps to millions, of people. Why not turn your attention to the development of aerial transportation, instead of competing with J.J. Hill and others for a chance in the steam railway world?

It is quite true that if you are a workman in the employ of the steel trust you have very little chance of becoming the owner of the plant in which you work; but it is also true that if you will commence to act in a Certain Way, you can soon leave the employ of the steel trust; you can buy a farm of from ten to forty acres, and engage in business as a producer of foodstuffs. There is great opportunity at this time for men who will live upon small tracts of land and cultivate the same intensively; such men will certainly get rich. You may say that it is impossible for you to get the land, but I am going to prove to you that it is not impossible, and that you can certainly get a farm if you will go to work in a Certain Way.

At different periods the tide of opportunity sets in different directions, according to the needs of the whole, and the particular stage of social evolution which has been reached. At present, in America, it is setting toward agriculture and the allied industries and professions. To-day, opportunity is open before the factory worker in his line. It is open before the business man who supplies the farmer more than before the one who supplies the factory worker; and before the professional man who waits upon the farmer more than before the one who serves the working class.

There is abundance of opportunity for the man who will go

with the tide, instead of trying to swim against it.

So the factory workers, either as individuals or as a class, are not deprived of opportunity. The workers are not being "kept down" by their masters; they are not being "ground" by the trusts and combinations of capital. As a class, they are where they are because they do not do things in a Certain Way. If the workers of America chose to do so, they could follow the example of their brothers in Belgium and other countries, and establish great department stores and co-operative industries; they could elect men of their own class to office, and pass laws favoring the development of such co-operative industries; and in a few years they could take peaceable possession of the industrial field.

The working class may become the master class whenever they will begin to do things in a Certain Way; the law of wealth is the same for them as it is for all others. This they must learn; and they will remain where they are as long as they continue to do as they do. The individual worker, however, is not held down by the ignorance or the mental slothfulness of his class; he can follow the tide of opportunity to riches, and this book will tell him how.

No one is kept in poverty by a shortness in the supply of riches; there is more than enough for all. A palace as large as the capitol at Washington might be built for every family on earth from the building material in the United States alone; and under intensive cultivation, this country would produce wool, cotton, linen, and silk enough to cloth each person in the world finer than Solomon was arrayed in all his glory; together with food enough to feed them all luxuriously.

The visible supply is practically inexhaustible; and the invisible supply really IS inexhaustible.

Everything you see on earth is made from one original substance, out of which all things proceed.

New Forms are constantly being made, and older ones are dissolving; but all are shapes assumed by One Thing.

There is no limit to the supply of Formless Stuff, or Original Substance. The universe is made out of it; but it was not all used in making the universe. The spaces in, through, and between the forms of the visible universe are permeated and filled with the Original Substance; with the formless Stuff; with the raw material of all things. Ten thousand times as much as has been made might still be made, and even then we should not have exhausted the supply of universal raw material.

No man, therefore, is poor because nature is poor, or because there is not enough to go around.

Nature is an inexhaustible storehouse of riches; the supply will never run short. Original Substance is alive with creative energy, and is constantly producing more forms. When the supply of building material is exhausted, more will be produced; when the soil is exhausted so that food stuffs and materials for clothing will no longer grow upon it, it will be renewed or more soil will be made. When all the gold and silver has been dug from the earth, if man is still in such a stage of social development that he needs gold and silver, more will produced from the Formless. The Formless Stuff responds to the needs of man; it will not let him be without any good thing.

This is true of man collectively; the race as a whole is always abundantly rich, and if individuals are poor, it is because they do not follow the Certain Way of doing things which makes the individual man rich.

The Formless Stuff is intelligent; it is stuff which thinks. It is alive, and is always impelled toward more life.

It is the natural and inherent impulse of life to seek to live more; it is the nature of intelligence to enlarge itself, and of consciousness to seek to extend its boundaries and find fuller expression. The universe of forms has been made by Formless Living Substance, throwing itself into form in order to express itself more fully.

The universe is a great Living Presence, always moving inherently toward more life and fuller functioning.

Nature is formed for the advancement of life; its impelling motive is the increase of life. For this cause, everything which can possibly minister to life is bountifully provided; there can be no lack unless God is to contradict himself and nullify his own works.

You are not kept poor by lack in the supply of riches; it is a fact which I shall demonstrate a little farther on that even the resources of the Formless Supply are at the command of the man or woman will act and think in a Certain Way.

CHAPTER 4

The First Principle in *The Science of Getting Rich*

THOUGHT is the only power which can produce tangible riches from the Formless Substance. The stuff from which all things are made is a substance which thinks, and a thought of form in this substance produces the form.

Original Substance moves according to its thoughts; every form and process you see in nature is the visible expression of a thought in Original Substance. As the Formless Stuff thinks of a form, it takes that form; as it thinks of a motion, it makes that motion. That is the way all things were created. We live in a thought world, which is part of a thought universe. The thought of a moving universe extended throughout Formless Substance, and the Thinking Stuff moving according to that thought, took the form of systems of planets, and maintains that form. Thinking Substance takes the form of its thought, and moves according to the thought. Holding the idea of a circling system of suns and worlds, it takes the form of these bodies, and moves them as it thinks. Thinking the form of a slow-growing oak tree, it moves accordingly, and produces the tree, though centuries may be required to do the work. In creating, the Formless seems to move according to the lines of motion it has established; the thought of an oak tree does not cause the instant formation of a full-grown tree, but it does start in motion the forces which will produce the tree, along established lines of growth.

Every thought of form, held in thinking Substance, causes the creation of the form, but always, or at least generally, along lines of growth and action already established.

The thought of a house of a certain construction, if it were impressed upon Formless Substance, might not cause the instant formation, of the house; but it would cause the turning of creative energies already working in trade and commerce into such channels as to result in the speedy building of the house. And if there were no existing channels through which the creative energy could work, then the house would be formed directly from primal substance, without waiting for the slow processes of the organic and inorganic world.

No thought of form can be impressed upon Original Substance without causing the creation of the form.

Man is a thinking center, and can originate thought. All the forms that man fashions with his hands must first exist in his thought; he cannot shape a thing until he has thought that thing.

And so far man has confined his efforts wholly to the work of his hands; he has applied manual labor to the world of forms, seeking to change or modify those already existing. He has never thought of trying to cause the creation of new forms by impressing his thoughts upon Formless Substance.

When man has a thought-form, he takes material from the forms of nature, and makes an image of the form which is in his mind. He has, so far, made little or no effort to co-operate with Formless Intelligence; to work "with the Father." He has not dreamed that he can "do what he seeth the Father doing." Man reshapes and modifies existing forms by manual labor; he has given no attention to the question whether he may not produce things from Formless Substance by communicating his thoughts to it. We propose to prove that he may do so; to prove that any man or woman may do so, and to show how. As our first step, we must lay down three fundamental propositions.

First, we assert that there is one original formless stuff, or substance, from which all things are made. All the seemingly many elements are but different presentations of one element; all the many forms found in organic and inorganic nature are but different shapes, made from the same stuff. And this stuff is thinking stuff; a thought held in it produces the form of the thought. Thought, in thinking substance, produces shapes. Man is a thinking center, capable of original thought; if man can communicate his thought to original thinking substance, he can cause the creation, or formation, of the thing he thinks about. To summarize this:

There is a thinking stuff from which all things are made, and which, in its original state, permeates, penetrates, and fills the interspaces of the universe.

A thought, in this substance, Produces the thing that is imaged by the thought.

Man can form things in his thought, and, by impressing his

thought upon formless substance, can cause the thing he thinks about to be created.

It may be asked if I can prove these statements; and without going into details, I answer that I can do so, both by logic and experience.

Reasoning back from the phenomena of form and thought, I come to one original thinking substance; and reasoning forward from this thinking substance, I come to man's power to cause the formation of the thing he thinks about.

And by experiment, I find the reasoning true; and this is my strongest proof.

If one man who reads this book gets rich by doing what it tells him to do, that is evidence in support of my claim; but if every man who does what it tells him to do gets rich, that is positive proof until some one goes through the process and fails. The theory is true until the process fails; and this process will not fail, for every man who does exactly what this book tells him to do will get rich.

I have said that men get rich by doing things in a Certain Way; and in order to do so, men must become able to think in a certain way.

A man's way of doing things is the direct result of the way he thinks about things.

To do things in a way you want to do them, you will have to acquire the ability to think the way you want to think; this is the first step toward getting rich.

To think what you want to think is to think TRUTH, regardless of appearances.

Every man has the natural and inherent power to think what he wants to think, but it requires far more effort to do so than it does to think the thoughts which are suggested by appearances. To think according to appearance is easy; to think truth regardless of appearances is laborious, and requires the expenditure of more power than any other work man is called upon to perform.

There is no labor from which most people shrink as they do from that of sustained and consecutive thought; it is the hardest work in the world. This is especially true when truth is contrary to appearances. Every appearance in the visible world tends to produce a corresponding form in the mind which observes it; and this can only be prevented by holding the thought of the TRUTH.

To look upon the appearance of disease will produce the form of disease in your own mind, and ultimately in your body, unless you hold the thought of the truth, which is that there is no disease; it is only an appearance, and the reality is health.

To look upon the appearances of poverty will produce corresponding forms in your own mind, unless you hold to the truth that there is no poverty; there is only abundance.

To think health when surrounded by the appearances of disease, or to think riches when in the midst of appearances of poverty, requires power; but he who acquires this power becomes a MASTER MIND. He can conquer fate; he can have what he wants.

This power can only be acquired by getting hold of the basic fact which is behind all appearances; and that fact is that there is one Thinking Substance, from which and by which all things are made.

Then we must grasp the truth that every thought held in this substance becomes a form, and that man can so impress his thoughts upon it as to cause them to take form and become visible things.

When we realize this, we lose all doubt and fear, for we know that we can create what we want to create; we can get what we want to have, and can become what we want to be. As a first step toward getting rich, you must believe the three fundamental statements given previously in this chapter; and in order to emphasize them. I repeat them here:

There is a thinking stuff from which all things are made, and which, in its original state, permeates, penetrates, and fills the interspaces of the universe.

A thought, in this substance, Produces the thing that is imaged by the thought.

Man can form things in his thought, and, by impressing his thought upon formless substance, can cause the thing he thinks about to be created.

You must lay aside all other concepts of the universe than this monistic one; and you must dwell upon this until it is fixed in your mind, and has become your habitual thought. Read these creed statements over and over again; fix every word upon your memory, and meditate upon them until you firmly believe what they say. If a doubt comes to you, cast it aside as a sin. Do not listen to arguments against this idea; do not go to churches or lectures where a contrary concept of things is taught or preached. Do not read magazines or books which teach a different idea; if you get mixed up in your faith, all your efforts will be in vain.

Do not ask why these things are true, nor speculate as to how they can be true; simply take them on trust.

The science of getting rich begins with the absolute acceptance of this faith.

CHAPTER 5

Increasing Life

YOU must get rid of the last vestige of the old idea that there is a Deity whose will it is that you should be poor, or whose purposes may be served by keeping you in poverty.

The Intelligent Substance which is All, and in All, and which lives in All and lives in you, is a consciously Living Substance. Being a consciously living substance, It must have the nature and inherent desire of every living intelligence for increase of life. Every living thing must continually seek for the enlargement of its life, because life, in the mere act of living, must increase itself.

A seed, dropped into the ground, springs into activity, and in the act of living produces a hundred more seeds; life, by living, multiplies itself. It is forever Becoming More; it must do so, if it continues to be at all.

Intelligence is under this same necessity for continuous increase. Every thought we think makes it necessary for us to think another thought; consciousness is continually expanding. Every fact we learn leads us to the learning of another fact; knowledge is continually increasing. Every talent we cultivate brings to the mind the desire to cultivate another talent; we are subject to the urge of life, seeking expression, which ever drives us on to know more, to do more, and to be more.

In order to know more, do more, and be more we must have more; we must have things to use, for we learn, and do, and become, only by using things. We must get rich, so that we can live more.

The desire for riches is simply the capacity for larger life seeking fulfillment; every desire is the effort of an unexpressed possibility to come into action. It is power seeking to manifest which causes desire. That which makes you want more money is the same as that which makes the plant grow; it is Life, seeking fuller expression.

The One Living Substance must be subject to this inherent law of all life; it is permeated with the desire to live more; that is why it is under the necessity of creating things.

The One Substance desires to live more in you; hence it wants you to have all the things you can use.

It is the desire of God that you should get rich. He wants you to get rich because he can express himself better through you if you have plenty of things to use in giving him expression. He can live more in you if you have unlimited command of the means of life.

The universe desires you to have everything you want to have.

Nature is friendly to your plans.

Everything is naturally for you.

Make up your mind that this is true.

It is essential, however that your purpose should harmonize with the purpose that is in All.

You must want real life, not mere pleasure of sensual gratification. Life is the performance of function; and the individual really lives only when he performs every function, physical, mental, and spiritual, of which he is capable, without excess in any.

You do not want to get rich in order to live swinishly, for the gratification of animal desires; that is not life. But the performance of every physical function is a part of life, and no one lives completely who denies the impulses of the body a normal and healthful expression.

You do not want to get rich solely to enjoy mental pleasures, to get knowledge, to gratify ambition, to outshine others, to be famous. All these are a legitimate part of life, but the man who lives for the pleasures of the intellect alone will only have a partial life, and he will never be satisfied with his lot.

You do not want to get rich solely for the good of others, to lose yourself for the salvation of mankind, to experience the joys of philanthropy and sacrifice. The joys of the soul are only a part of life; and they are no better or nobler than any other part.

You want to get rich in order that you may eat, drink, and be merry when it is time to do these things; in order that you may surround yourself with beautiful things, see distant lands, feed your mind, and develop your intellect; in order that you may love men and do kind things, and be able to play a good part in helping the world to find truth.

But remember that extreme altruism is no better and no nobler than extreme selfishness; both are mistakes.

Get rid of the idea that God wants you to sacrifice yourself for others, and that you can secure his favor by doing so; God requires nothing of the kind.

What he wants is that you should make the most of yourself, for yourself, and for others; and you can help others more by making the most of yourself than in any other way.

You can make the most of yourself only by getting rich; so it is right and praiseworthy that you should give your first and best thought to the work of acquiring wealth.

Remember, however, that the desire of Substance is for all, and its movements must be for more life to all; it cannot be made to work for less life to any, because it is equally in all, seeking riches and life.

Intelligent Substance will make things for you, but it will not take things away from some one else and give them to you.

You must get rid of the thought of competition. You are to create, not to compete for what is already created.

You do not have to take anything away from any one.

You do not have to drive sharp bargains.

You do not have to cheat, or to take advantage. You do not need to let any man work for you for less than he earns.

You do not have to covet the property of others, or to look at it with wishful eyes; no man has anything of which you cannot have the like, and that without taking what he has away from him.

You are to become a creator, not a competitor; you are going to get what you want, but in such a way that when you get it every other man will have more than he has now.

I am aware that there are men who get a vast amount of money by proceeding in direct opposition to the statements in the paragraph above, and may add a word of explanation here. Men of the plutocratic type, who become very rich, do so sometimes purely by their extraordinary ability on the plane of competition; and sometimes they unconsciously relate themselves to Substance in its great purposes and movements for the general racial upbuilding through industrial evolution. Rockefeller, Carnegie, Morgan, et al., have been the unconscious agents of the Supreme in the necessary work of systematizing and organizing productive industry; and in the end, their work will contribute immensely toward increased life for all. Their day is nearly over; they have organized production, and will soon be succeeded by the agents of the multitude, who will organize the machinery of distribution.

The multi-millionaires are like the monster reptiles of the prehistoric eras; they play a necessary part in the evolutionary process, but the same Power which produced them will dispose of them. And it is well to bear in mind that they have never been really rich; a record of the private lives of most of this class will show that they have really been the most abject and wretched of the poor.

Riches secured on the competitive plane are never satisfactory and permanent; they are yours to-day, and another's tomorrow. Remember, if you are to become rich in a scientific and certain way, you must rise entirely out of the competitive thought. You must never think for a moment that the supply is limited. Just as soon as you begin to think that all the money is being "cornered" and controlled by bankers and others, and that you must exert yourself to get laws passed to stop this process, and so on; in that moment you drop into the competitive mind, and your power to cause creation is gone for the time being; and what is worse, you will probably arrest the creative movements you have already instituted.

KNOW that there are countless millions of dollars' worth of gold in the mountains of the earth, not yet brought to light; and know that if there were not, more would be created from Thinking Substance to supply your needs.

KNOW that the money you need will come, even if it is necessary for a thousand men to be led to the discovery of new gold mines to-morrow.

Never look at the visible supply; look always at the limitless riches in Formless Substance, and KNOW that they are coming to you as fast as you can receive and use them. Nobody, by cornering the visible supply, can prevent you from getting what is yours.

So never allow yourself to think for an instant that all the best building spots will be taken before you get ready to build your house, unless you hurry. Never worry about the trusts and combines, and get anxious for fear they will soon come to own the whole earth. Never get afraid that you will lose what you want because some other person "beats you to it." That cannot possibly happen; you are not seeking any thing that is possessed by anybody else; you are causing what you want to be created from formless Substance, and the supply is without limits. Stick to the formulated statement:

There is a thinking stuff from which all things are made, and which, in its original state, permeates, penetrates, and fills the interspaces of the universe.

A thought, in this substance, produces the thing that is imaged by the thought.

Man can form things in his thought, and, by impressing his thought upon formless substance, can cause the thing he thinks about to be created.

CHAPTER 6

How Riches Come to You

WHEN I say that you do not have to drive sharp bargains, I do not mean that you do not have to drive any bargains at all, or that you are above the necessity for having any dealings with your fellow men. I mean that you will not need to deal with them unfairly; you do not have to get something for nothing, but can give to every man more than you take from him.

You cannot give every man more in cash market value than you take from him, but you can give him more in use value than the cash value of the thing you take from him. The paper, ink, and other material in this book may not be worth the money you pay for it; but if the ideas suggested by it bring you thousands of dollars, you have not been wronged by those who sold it to you; they have given you a great use value for a small cash value.

Let us suppose that I own a picture by one of the great artists, which, in any civilized community, is worth thousands of dollars. I take it to Baffin Ray, and by "salesmanship" induce an Eskimo to give a bundle of furs worth $ 500 for it. I have really wronged him, for he has no use for the picture; it has no use value to him; it will not add to his life.

But suppose I give him a gun worth $50 for his furs; then he has made a good bargain. He has use for the gun; it will get him many more furs and much food; it will add to his life in every way; it will make him rich.

When you rise from the competitive to the creative plane, you can scan your business transactions very strictly, and if you are selling any man anything which does not add more to his life than the thing he give you in exchange, you can afford to stop it. You do not have to beat anybody in business. And if you are in a business which does beat people, get out of it at once.

Give every man more in use value than you take from him in cash value; then you are adding to the life of the world by every business transaction.

If you have people working for you, you must take from them more in cash value than you pay them in wages; but you can so organize your business that it will be filled with the principle of advancement, and so that each employee who wishes to do so may advance a little every day.

You can make your business do for your employees what this book is doing for you. You can so conduct your business that it will be a sort of ladder, by which every employee who will take the trouble may climb to riches himself; and given the opportunity, if he will not do so it is not your fault.

And finally, because you are to cause the creation of your riches from Formless Substance which permeates all your environment, it does not follow that they are to take shape from the atmosphere and come into being before your eyes.

If you want a sewing machine, for instance, I do not mean to tell you that you are to impress the thought of a sewing machine on Thinking Substance until the machine is formed without hands, in the room where you sit, or elsewhere. But if you want a sewing machine, hold the mental image of it with the most positive certainty that it is being made, or is on its way to you. After once forming the thought, have the most absolute and unquestioning faith that the sewing machine is coming; never think of it, or speak, of it, in any other way than as being sure to arrive. Claim it as already yours.

It will be brought to you by the power of the Supreme Intelligence, acting upon the minds of men. If you live in Maine, it may be that a man will be brought from Texas or Japan to engage in some transaction which will result in your getting what you want.

If so, the whole matter will be as much to that man's advantage as it is to yours.

Do not forget for a moment that the Thinking Substance is through all, in all, communicating with all, and can influence all. The desire of Thinking Substance for fuller life and better living has caused the creation of all the sewing machines already made; and it can cause the creation of millions more, and will, whenever men set it in motion by desire and faith, and by acting in a Certain Way.

You can certainly have a sewing machine in your house; and it is just as certain that you can have any other thing or things which you want, and which you will use for the advancement of your own life and the lives of others.

You need not hesitate about asking largely; "it is your Father's pleasure to give you the kingdom," said Jesus.

Original Substance wants to live all that is possible in you, and wants you to have all that you can or will use for the living of the most abundant life.

If you fix upon your consciousness the fact that the desire you feel for the possession of riches is one with the desire of Omnipotence for more complete expression, your faith becomes invincible.

Once I saw a little boy sitting at a piano, and vainly trying to bring harmony out of the keys; and I saw that he was grieved and provoked by his inability to play real music. I asked him the cause of his vexation, and he answered, "I can feel the music in me, but I can't make my hands go right." The music in him was the URGE of Original Substance, containing all the possibilities of all life; all that there is of music was seeking expression through the child.

God, the One Substance, is trying to live and do and enjoy things through humanity. He is saying "I want hands to build wonderful structures, to play divine harmonies, to paint glorious pictures; I want feet to run my errands, eyes to see my beauties, tongues to tell mighty truths and to sing marvelous songs," and so on.

All that there is of possibility is seeking expression through men. God wants those who can play music to have pianos and every other instrument, and to have the means to cultivate their talents to the fullest extent; He wants those who can appreciate beauty to be able to surround themselves with beautiful things; He wants those who can discern truth to have every opportunity to travel and observe; He wants those who can appreciate dress to be beautifully clothed, and those who can appreciate good food to be luxuriously fed.

He wants all these things because it is Himself that enjoys and appreciates them; it is God who wants to play, and sing, and enjoy beauty, and proclaim truth and wear fine clothes, and eat good foods. "it is God that worketh in you to will and to do," said Paul.

The desire you feel for riches is the infinite, seeking to express Himself in you as He sought to find expression in the little boy at the piano.

So you need not hesitate to ask largely.

Your part is to focalize and express the desire to God.

This is a difficult point with most people; they retain something of the old idea that poverty and self-sacrifice are pleasing to God. They look upon poverty as a part of the plan, a necessity of nature. They have the idea that God has finished His work, and made all that He can make, and that the majority of men must stay poor because there is not enough to go around. They hold to so much of this erroneous thought that they feel ashamed to ask for wealth; they try not to want more than a very modest competence, just enough to make them fairly comfortable.

I recall now the case of one student who was told that he must get in mind a clear picture of the things he desired, so that the creative thought of them might be impressed on Formless Substance. He was a very poor man, living in a rented house, and having only what he earned from day to day; and he could not grasp the fact that all wealth was his. So, after thinking the matter over, he decided that he might reasonably ask for a new rug for the floor of his best room, and an anthracite coal stove to heat the house during the cold weather. Following the instructions given in this book, he obtained these things in a few months; and then it dawned upon him that he had not asked enough. He went through the house in which he lived, and planned all the improvements he would like to make in it; he mentally added a bay window here and a room there, until it was complete in his mind as his ideal home; and then he planned its furnishings.

Holding the whole picture in his mind, he began living in the Certain Way, and moving toward what he wanted; and he owns the house now, and is rebuilding it after the form of his mental image. And now, with still larger faith, he is going on to get greater things. It has been unto him according to his faith, and it is so with you and with all of us.

CHAPTER 7

Gratitude

THE illustrations given in the last chapter will have conveyed to the reader the fact that the first step toward getting rich is to convey the idea of your wants to the Formless Substance.

This is true, and you will see that in order to do so it becomes necessary to relate yourself to the Formless Intelligence in a harmonious way.

To secure this harmonious relation is a matter of such primary and vital importance that I shall give some space to its discussion here, and give you instructions which, if you will follow them, will be certain to bring you into perfect unity of mind with God.

The whole process of mental adjustment and atonement can be summed up in one word, gratitude.

First, you believe that there is one Intelligent Substance, from which all things proceed; second, you believe that this Substance gives you everything you desire; and third, you relate yourself to it by a feeling of deep and profound gratitude.

Many people who order their lives rightly in all other ways are kept in poverty by their lack of gratitude. Having received one gift from God, they cut the wires which connect them with Him by failing to make acknowledgment.

It is easy to understand that the nearer we live to the source of wealth, the more wealth we shall receive; and it is easy also to understand that the soul that is always grateful lives in closer touch with God than the one which never looks to Him in thankful acknowledgment.

The more gratefully we fix our minds on the Supreme when good things come to us, the more good things we will receive, and the more rapidly they will come; and the reason simply is that the mental attitude of gratitude draws the mind into closer touch with the source from which the blessings come.

If it is a new thought to you that gratitude brings your whole mind into closer harmony with the creative energies of the universe, consider it well, and you will see that it is true. The good things you already have have come to you along the line of obedience to certain laws. Gratitude will lead your mind out along the ways by which things come; and it will keep you in close harmony with creative thought and prevent you from falling into competitive thought.

Gratitude alone can keep you looking toward the All, and prevent you from falling into the error of thinking of the supply as limited; and to do that would be fatal to your hopes.

There is a Law of Gratitude, and it is absolutely necessary that you should observe the law, if you are to get the results you seek.

The law of gratitude is the natural principle that action and reaction are always equal, and in opposite directions.

The grateful outreaching of your mind in thankful praise to the Supreme is a liberation or expenditure of force; it cannot fail to reach that to which it addressed, and the reaction is an instantaneous movement towards you.

"Draw nigh unto God, and He will draw nigh unto you." That is a statement of psychological truth.

And if your gratitude is strong and constant, the reaction in Formless Substance will be strong and continuous; the movement of the things you want will be always toward you. Notice the grateful attitude that Jesus took; how He always seems to be saying, "I thank Thee, Father, that Thou hearest me." You cannot exercise much power without gratitude; for it is gratitude that keeps you connected with Power.

But the value of gratitude does not consist solely in getting you more blessings in the future. Without gratitude you cannot long keep from dissatisfied thought regarding things as they are.

The moment you permit your mind to dwell with dissatisfaction upon things as they are, you begin to lose ground. You fix attention upon the common, the ordinary, the poor, and the squalid and mean; and your mind takes the form of these things. Then you will transmit these forms or mental images to the Formless, and the common, the poor, the squalid, and mean will come to you.

To permit your mind to dwell upon the inferior is to become inferior and to surround yourself with inferior things.

On the other hand, to fix your attention on the best is to surround yourself with the best, and to become the best.

The Creative Power within us makes us into the image of that to which we give our attention.

We are Thinking Substance, and thinking substance always takes the form of that which it thinks about.

The grateful mind is constantly fixed upon the best; therefore it tends to become the best; it takes the form or character of the best, and will receive the best.

Also, faith is born of gratitude. The grateful mind continually expects good things, and expectation becomes faith. The reaction of gratitude upon one's own mind produces faith; and every outgoing wave of grateful thanksgiving increases faith. He who has no feeling of gratitude cannot long retain a living faith; and without a living faith you cannot get rich by the creative method, as we shall see in the following chapters.

It is necessary, then, to cultivate the habit of being grateful for every good thing that comes to you; and to give thanks continuously.

And because all things have contributed to your advancement, you should include all things in your gratitude.

Do not waste time thinking or talking about the shortcomings or wrong actions of plutocrats or trust magnates. Their organization of the world has made your opportunity; all you get really comes to you because of them.

Do not rage against, corrupt politicians; if it were not for politicians we should fall into anarchy, and your opportunity would be greatly lessened.

God has worked a long time and very patiently to bring us up to where we are in industry and government, and He is going right on with His work. There is not the least doubt that He will do away with plutocrats, trust magnates, captains of industry, and politicians as soon as they can be spared; but in the meantime, behold they are all very good. Remember that they are all helping to arrange the lines of transmission along which your riches will come to you, and be grateful to them all. This will bring you into harmonious relations with the good in everything, and the good in everything will move toward you.

CHAPTER 8

Thinking in the Certain Way

TURN back to chapter 6 and read again the story of the man who formed a mental image of his house, and you will get a fair idea of the initial step toward getting rich. You must form a clear and definite mental picture of what you want; you cannot transmit an idea unless you have it yourself.

You must have it before you can give it; and many people fail to impress Thinking Substance because they have themselves only a vague and misty concept of the things they want to do, to have, or to become.

It is not enough that you should have a general desire for wealth "to do good with"; everybody has that desire.

It is not enough that you should have a wish to travel, see things, live more, etc. Everybody has those desires also. If you were going to send a wireless message to a friend, you would not send the letters of the alphabet in their order, and let him construct the message for himself; nor would you take words at random from the dictionary. You would send a coherent sentence; one which meant something. When you try to impress your wants upon Substance, remember that it must be done by a coherent statement; you must know what you want, and be definite. You can never get rich, or start the creative power into action, by sending out unformed longings and vague desires.

Go over your desires just as the man I have described went over his house; see just what you want, and get a clear mental picture of it as you wish it to look when you get it.

That clear mental picture you must have continually in mind, as the sailor has in mind the port toward which he is sailing the ship; you must keep your face toward it all the time. You must no more lose sight of it than the steersman loses sight of the compass.

It is not necessary to take exercises in concentration, nor to set apart special times for prayer and affirmation, nor to "go into the silence," nor to do occult stunts of any kind. Those things are well enough, but all you need is to know what you want, and to want it badly enough so that it will stay in your thoughts.

Spend as much of your leisure time as you can in contemplating your picture, but no one needs to take exercises to concentrate his mind on a thing which he really wants; it is the things you do not really care about which require effort to fix your attention upon them.

And unless you really want to get rich, so that the desire is strong enough to hold your thoughts directed to the purpose as the magnetic pole holds the needle of the compass, it will hardly be worth while for you to try to carry out the instructions given in this book.

The methods herein set forth are for people whose desire for riches is strong enough to overcome mental laziness and the love of ease, and make them work.

The more clear and definite you make your picture then, and the more you dwell upon it, bringing out all its delightful details, the stronger your desire will be; and the stronger your desire, the easier it will be to hold your mind fixed upon the picture of what you want.

Something more is necessary, however, than merely to see the picture clearly. If that is all you do, you are only a dreamer, and will have little or no power for accomplishment.

Behind your clear vision must be the purpose to realize it; to bring it out in tangible expression.

And behind this purpose must be an invincible and unwavering FAITH that the thing is already yours; that it is "at hand" and you have only to take possession of it.

Live in the new house, mentally, until it takes form around you physically. In the mental realm, enter at once into full enjoyment of the things you want.

"Whatsoever things ye ask for when ye pray, believe that ye receive them, and ye shall have them," said Jesus.

See the things you want as if they were actually around you all the time; see yourself as owning and using them. Make use of them in imagination just as you will use them when they are your tangible possessions. Dwell upon your mental picture until it is clear and distinct, and then take the Mental Attitude of Ownership toward everything in that picture. Take possession of it, in mind, in the full faith that it is actually yours. Hold to this mental ownership; do not waiver for an instant in the faith that it is real.

And remember what was said in a proceeding chapter about gratitude; be as thankful for it all the time as you expect to be when it has taken form. The man who can sincerely thank God for the things which as yet he owns only in imagination, has real faith. He will get rich; he will cause the creation of whatsoever he wants.

You do not need to pray repeatedly for things you want; it is not necessary to tell God about it every day.

"Use not vain repetitions as the heathen do," said Jesus to his pupils, "for your Father knoweth the ye have need of these things before ye ask Him."

Your part is to intelligently formulate your desire for the things which make for a larger life, and to get these desires arranged into a coherent whole; and then to impress this Whole Desire upon the Formless Substance, which has the power and the will to bring you what you want.

You do not make this impression by repeating strings of words; you make it by holding the vision with unshakable PURPOSE to attain it, and with steadfast FAITH that you do attain it.

The answer to prayer is not according to your faith while you are talking, but according to your faith while you are working.

You cannot impress the mind of God by having a special Sabbath day set apart to tell Him what you want, and then forgetting Him during the rest of the week. You cannot impress Him by having special hours to go into your closet and pray, if you then dismiss the matter from your mind until the hour of prayer comes again.

Oral prayer is well enough, and has its effect, especially upon yourself, in clarifying your vision and strengthening your faith; but it is not your oral petitions which get you what you want. In order to get rich you do not need a "sweet hour of prayer"; you need to "pray without ceasing." And by prayer I mean holding steadily to your vision, with the purpose to cause its creation into solid form, and the faith that you are doing so.

"Believe that ye receive them."

The whole matter turns on receiving, once you have clearly formed your vision. When you have formed it, it is well to make an oral statement, addressing the Supreme in reverent prayer; and from that moment you must, in mind, receive what you ask for. Live in the new house; wear the fine clothes; ride in the automobile; go on the journey, and confidently plan for greater journeys. Think and speak of all the things you have asked for in terms of actual present ownership. Imagine an environment, and a financial condition exactly as you want them, and live all the time in that imaginary environment and financial condition. Mind, however, that you do not do this as a mere dreamer and castle builder; hold to the FAITH that the imaginary is being realized, and to the PURPOSE to realize it. Remember that it is faith and purpose in the use of the imagination which make the difference between the scientist and the dreamer. And having learned this fact, it is here that you must learn the proper use of the Will.

CHAPTER 9

How to Use the Will

TO set about getting rich in a scientific way, you do not try to apply your will power to anything outside of yourself.

You have no right to do so, anyway.

It is wrong to apply your will to other men and women, in order to get them to do what you wish done.

It is as flagrantly wrong to coerce people by mental power as it is to coerce them by physical power. If compelling people by physical force to do things for you reduces them to slavery, compelling them by mental means accomplishes exactly the same thing; the only difference is in methods. If taking things from people by physical force is robbery, them taking things by mental force is robbery also; there is no difference in principle.

You have no right to use your will power upon another person, even "for his own good"; for you do not know what is for his good. The science of getting rich does not require you to apply power or force to any other person, in any way whatsoever. There is not the slightest necessity for doing so; indeed, any attempt to use your will upon others will only tend to defeat your purpose.

You do not need to apply your will to things, in order to compel them to come to you.

That would simply be trying to coerce God, and would be foolish and useless, as well as irreverent.

You do not have to compel God to give you good things, any more than you have to use your will power to make the sun rise.

You do not have to use your will power to conquer an unfriendly deity, or to make stubborn and rebellious forces do your bidding.

Substance is friendly to you, and is more anxious to give you what you want than you are to get it.

To get rich, you need only to use your will power upon yourself.

When you know what to think and do, then you must use your will to compel yourself to think and do the right things. That is the legitimate use of the will in getting what you want—to use it in holding yourself to the right course. Use your will to keep yourself thinking and acting in the Certain Way.

Do not try to project your will, or your thoughts, or your mind out into space, to "act" on things or people.

Keep your mind at home; it can accomplish more there than elsewhere.

Use your mind to form a mental image of what you want, and to hold that vision with faith and purpose; and use your will to keep your mind working in the Right Way.

The more steady and continuous your faith and purpose, the more rapidly you will get rich, because you will make only POSITIVE impressions upon Substance; and you will not neutralize or offset them by negative impressions.

The picture of your desires, held with faith and purpose, is taken up by the Formless, and permeates it to great distances— throughout the universe, for all I know.

As this impression spreads, all things are set moving toward its realization; every living thing, every inanimate thing, and the things yet uncreated, are stirred toward bringing into being that which you want. All force begins to be exerted in that direction; all things begin to move toward you. The minds of people, everywhere, are influenced toward doing the things necessary to the fulfilling of your desires; and they work for you, unconsciously.

But you can check all this by starting a negative impression in the Formless Substance. Doubt or unbelief is as certain to start a movement away from you as faith and purpose are to start one toward you. It is by not understanding this that most people who try to make use of "mental science" in getting rich make their failure. Every hour and moment you spend in giving heed to doubts and fears, every hour you spend in worry, every hour in which your soul is possessed by unbelief, sets a current away from you in the whole domain of intelligent Substance. All the promises are unto them that believe, and unto them only. Notice how insistent Jesus was upon this point of belief; and now you know the reason why.

Since belief is all important, it behooves you to guard your thoughts; and as your beliefs will be shaped to a very great extent by the things you observe and think about, it is important that you should command your attention.

And here the will comes into use; for it is by your will that you determine upon what things your attention shall be fixed.

If you want to become rich, you must not make a study of poverty.

Things are not brought into being by thinking about their opposites. Health is never to be attained by studying disease and thinking about disease; righteousness is not to be promoted by studying sin and thinking about sin; and no one ever got rich by studying poverty and thinking about poverty.

Medicine as a science of disease has increased disease; religion as a science of sin has promoted sin, and economics as a study of poverty will fill the world with wretchedness and want.

Do not talk about poverty; do not investigate it, or concern yourself with it. Never mind what its causes are; you have nothing to do with them.

What concerns you is the cure.

Do not spend your time in charitable work, or charity movements; all charity only tends to perpetuate the wretchedness it aims to eradicate.

I do not say that you should be hard hearted or unkind, and refuse to hear the cry of need; but you must not try to eradicate poverty in any of the conventional ways. Put poverty behind you, and put all that pertains to it behind you, and "make good."

Get rich; that is the best way you can help the poor.

And you cannot hold the mental image which is to make you rich if you fill your mind with pictures of poverty. Do not read books or papers which give circumstantial accounts of the wretchedness of the tenement dwellers, of the horrors of child labor, and so on. Do not read anything which fills your mind with gloomy images of want and suffering.

You cannot help the poor in the least by knowing about these things; and the wide-spread knowledge of them does not tend at all to do away with poverty.

What tends to do away with poverty is not the getting of pictures of poverty into your mind, but getting pictures of wealth into the minds of the poor.

You are not deserting the poor in their misery when you refuse to allow your mind to be filled with pictures of that misery.

Poverty can be done away with, not by increasing the number of well to do people who think about poverty, but by increasing the number of poor people who purpose with faith to get rich.

The poor do not need charity; they need inspiration. Charity only sends them a loaf of bread to keep them alive in their wretchedness, or gives them an entertainment to make them forget for an hour or two; but inspiration will cause them to rise out of their misery. If you want to help the poor, demonstrate to them that they can become rich; prove it by getting rich yourself.

The only way in which poverty will ever be banished from this world is by getting a large and constantly increasing number of people to practice the teachings of this book.

People must be taught to become rich by creation, not by competition.

Every man who becomes rich by competition throws down behind him the ladder by which he rises, and keeps others down; but every man who gets rich by creation opens a way for thousands to follow him, and inspires them to do so.

You are not showing hardness of heart or an unfeeling disposition when you refuse to pity poverty, see poverty, read about poverty, or think or talk about it, or to listen to those who do talk about it. Use your will power to keep your mind OFF the subject of poverty, and to keep it fixed with faith and purpose ON the vision of what you want.

CHAPTER 10

Further Use of the Will

YOU cannot retain a true and clear vision of wealth if you are constantly turning your attention to opposing pictures, whether they be external or imaginary.

Do not tell of your past troubles of a financial nature, if you have had them, do not think of them at all. Do no tell of the poverty of your parents, or the hardships of your early life; to do any of these things is to mentally class yourself with the poor for the time being, and it will certainly check the movement of things in your direction.

"Let the dead bury their dead," as Jesus said.

Put poverty and all things that pertain to poverty completely behind you.

You have accepted a certain theory of the universe as being correct, and are resting all your hopes of happiness on its being correct; and what can you gain by giving heed to conflicting theories?

Do not read religious books which tell you that the world is soon coming to an end; and do not read the writing of muck-rakers and pessimistic philosophers who tell you that it is going to the devil.

The world is not going to the devil; it is going to God.

It is wonderful Becoming.

True, there may be a good many things in existing conditions which are disagreeable; but what is the use of studying them when they are certainly passing away, and when the study of them only tends to check their passing and keep them with us? Why give time and attention to things which are being removed by evolutionary growth, when you can hasten their removal only by promoting the evolutionary growth as far as your part of it goes?

No matter how horrible in seeming may be the conditions in certain countries, sections, or places, you waste your time and destroy your own chances by considering them.

You should interest yourself in the world's becoming rich.

Think of the riches the world is coming into, instead of the poverty it is growing out of; and bear in mind that the only way in which you can assist the world in growing rich is by growing rich yourself through the creative method—not the competitive one.

Give your attention wholly to riches; ignore poverty.

Whenever you think or speak of those who are poor, think and speak of them as those who are becoming rich;as those who are to be congratulated rather than pitied. Then they and others will catch the inspiration, and begin to search for the way out.

Because I say that you are to give your whole time and mind and thought to riches, it does not follow that you are to be sordid or mean.

To become really rich is the noblest aim you can have in life, for it includes everything else.

On the competitive plane, the struggle to get rich is a Godless scramble for power over other men; but when we come into the creative mind, all this is changed.

All that is possible in the way of greatness and soul unfoldment, of service and lofty endeavor, comes by way of getting rich; all is made possible by the use of things.

If you lack for physical health, you will find that the attainment of it is conditional on your getting rich.

Only those who are emancipated from financial worry, and who have the means to live a care-free existence and follow hygienic practices, can have and retain health.

Moral and spiritual greatness is possible only to those who are above the competitive battle for existence; and only those who are becoming rich on the plane of creative thought are free from the degrading influences of competition. If your heart is set on domestic happiness, remember that love flourishes best where there is refinement, a high level of thought, and freedom from corrupting influences; and these are to be found only where riches are attained by the exercise of creative thought, without strife or rivalry.

You can aim at nothing so great or noble, I repeat, as to become rich; and you must fix your attention upon your mental picture of riches, to the exclusion of all that may tend to dim or obscure the vision.

You must learn to see the underlying TRUTH in all things; you must see beneath all seemingly wrong conditions the Great One Life ever moving forward toward fuller expression and more complete happiness.

It is the truth that there is no such thing as poverty; that there is only wealth.

Some people remain in poverty because they are ignorant of the fact that there is wealth for them; and these can best be taught by showing them the way to affluence in your own person and practice.

Others are poor because, while they feel that there is a way out, they are too intellectually indolent to put forth the mental effort necessary to find that way and travel it; and for these the very best thing you can do is to arouse their desire by showing them the happiness that comes from being rightly rich.

Others still are poor because, while they have some notion of science, they have become so swamped and lost in the maze of metaphysical and occult theories that they do not know which road to take. They try a mixture of many systems and fail in all. For these, again, the very best thing, to do is to show the right way in your own person and practice; an ounce of doing things is worth a pound of theorizing.

The very best thing you can do for the whole world is to make the most of yourself.

You can serve God and man in no more effective way than by getting rich; that is, if you get rich by the creative method and not by the competitive one.

Another thing. We assert that this book gives in detail the principles of the science of getting rich; and if that is true, you do not need to read any other book upon the subject. This may sound narrow and egotistical, but consider: there is no more scientific method of computation in mathematics than by addition, subtraction, multiplication, and division; no other method is possible. There can be but one shortest distance between two points. There is only one way to think scientifically, and that is to think in the way that leads by the most direct and simple route to the goal. No man has yet formulated a briefer or less complex "system" than the one set forth herein; it has been stripped of all non-essentials. When you commence on this, lay all others aside; put them out of your mind altogether.

Read this book every day; keep it with you; commit it to memory, and do not think about other "systems" and theories. If you do, you will begin to have doubts, and to be uncertain and wavering in your thought; and then you will begin to make failures.

After you have made good and become rich, you may study other systems as much as you please; but until you are quite sure that you have gained what you want, do not read anything on this line but this book, unless it be the authors mentioned in the Preface.

And read only the most optimistic comments on the world's news; those in harmony with your picture.

Also, postpone your investigations into the occult. Do not dabble in theosophy, Spiritualism, or kindred studies. It is very likely that the dead still live, and are near; but if they are, let them alone; mind your own business.

Wherever the spirits of the dead may be, they have their own work to do, and their own problems to solve; and we have no right to interfere with them. We cannot help them, and it is very doubtful whether they can help us, or whether we have any right to trespass upon their time if they can. Let the dead and the hereafter alone, and solve your own problem; get rich. If you begin to mix with the occult, you will start mental cross-currents which will surely bring your hopes to shipwreck. Now, this and the preceding chapters have brought us to the following statement of basic facts:

There is a thinking stuff from which all things are made, and which, in its original state, permeates, penetrates, and fills the interspaces of the universe.

A thought, in this substance, Produces the thing that is imaged by the thought.

Man can form things in his thought, and, by impressing his thought upon formless substance, can cause the thing he thinks about to be created.

In order to do this, man must pass from the competitive to the creative mind; he must form a clear mental picture of the things he wants, and hold this picture in his thoughts with the fixed PURPOSE to get what he wants, and the unwavering FAITH that he does get what he wants, closing his mind against all that may tend to shake his purpose, dim his vision, or quench his faith.

And in addition to all this, we shall now see that he must live and act in a Certain Way.

CHAPTER 11

Acting in the Certain Way

THOUGHT is the creative power, or the impelling force which causes the creative power to act; thinking in a Certain Way will bring riches to you, but you must not rely upon thought alone, paying no attention to personal action. That is the rock upon which many otherwise scientific metaphysical thinkers meet shipwreck—the failure to connect thought with personal action.

We have not yet reached the stage of development, even supposing such a stage to be possible, in which man can create directly from Formless Substance without nature's processes or the work of human hands; man must not only think, but his personal action must supplement his thought.

By thought you can cause the gold in the hearts of the mountains to be impelled toward you; but it will not mine itself, refine itself, coin itself into double eagles, and come rolling along the roads seeking its way into your pocket.

Under the impelling power of the Supreme Spirit, men's affairs will be so ordered that some one will be led to mine the gold for you; other men's business transactions will be so directed that the gold will be brought toward you, and you must so arrange your own business affairs that you may be able to receive it when it comes to you. Your thought makes all things, animate and inanimate, work to bring you what you want; but your personal activity must be such that you can rightly receive what you want when it reaches you. You are not to take it as charity, nor to steal it; you must give every man more in use value than he gives you in cash value.

The scientific use of thought consists in forming a clear and distinct mental image of what you want; in holding fast to the purpose to get what you want; and in realizing with grateful faith that you do get what you want.

Do not try to "project" your thought in any mysterious or occult way, with the idea of having it go out and do things for you; that is wasted effort, and will weaken your power to think with sanity.

The action of thought in getting rich is fully explained in the preceding chapters; your faith and purpose positively impress your vision upon Formless Substance, which has THE SAME DESIRE FOR MORE LIFE THAT YOU HAVE; and this vision, received from you, sets all the creative forces at work IN AND THROUGH THEIR REGULAR CHANNELS OF ACTION, but directed toward you.

It is not your part to guide or supervise the creative process; all you have to do with that is to retain your vision, stick to your purpose, and maintain your faith and gratitude.

But you must act in a Certain Way, so that you can appropriate what is yours when it comes to you; so that you can meet the things you have in your picture, and put them in their proper places as they arrive.

You can really see the truth of this. When things reach you, they will be in the hands of other men, who will ask an equivalent for them.

And you can only get what is yours by giving the other man what is his.

Your pocketbook is not going to be transformed into a Fortunata's purse, which shall be always full of money without effort on your part.

This is the crucial point in the science of getting rich; right here, where thought and personal action must be combined. There are very many people who, consciously or unconsciously, set the creative forces in action by the strength and persistence of their desires, but who remain poor because they do not provide for the reception of the thing they want when it comes.

By thought, the thing you want is brought to you; by action you receive it.

Whatever your action is to be, it is evident that you must act NOW. You cannot act in the past, and it is essential to the clearness of your mental vision that you dismiss the past from your mind. You cannot act in the future, for the future is not here yet. And you cannot tell how you will want to act in any future contingency until that contingency has arrived.

Because you are not in the right business, or the right environment now, do not think that you must postpone action until you get into the right business or environment. And do not spend time in the present taking thought as to the best course in possible future emergencies; have faith in your ability to meet any emergency when it arrives.

If you act in the present with your mind on the future, your present action will be with a divided mind, and will not be effective.

Put your whole mind into present action.

Do not give your creative impulse to Original Substance, and then sit down and wait for results; if you do, you will never get them. Act now. There is never any time but now, and there never will be any time but now. If you are ever to begin to make ready for the reception of what you want, you must begin now.

And your action, whatever it is, must most likely be in your present business or employment, and must be upon the persons and things in your present environment.

You cannot act where you are not; you cannot act where you have been, and you cannot act where you are going to be; you can act only where you are.

Do not bother as to whether yesterday's work was well done or ill done; do to-day's work well.

Do not try to do tomorrow's work now; there will be plenty of time to do that when you get to it.

Do not try, by occult or mystical means, to act on people or things that are out of your reach.

Do not wait for a change of environment, before you act; get a change of environment by action.

You can so act upon the environment in which you are now, as to cause yourself to be transferred to a better environment.

Hold with faith and purpose the vision of yourself in the better environment, but act upon your present environment with all your heart, and with all your strength, and with all your mind.

Do not spend any time in day dreaming or castle building; hold to the one vision of what you want, and act NOW.

Do not cast about seeking some new thing to do, or some strange, unusual, or remarkable action to perform as a first step toward getting rich. It is probable that your actions, at least for some time to come, will be those you have been performing for some time past; but you are to begin now to perform these actions in the Certain Way, which will surely make you rich.

If you are engaged in some business, and feel that it is not the right one for you, do not wait until you get into the right business before you begin to act.

Do not feel discouraged, or sit down and lament because you are misplaced. No man was ever so misplaced but that he could not find the right place, and no man ever became so involved in the wrong business but that he could get into the right business.

Hold the vision of yourself in the right business, with the purpose to get into it, and the faith that you will get into it, and are getting into it; but ACT in your present business. Use your present business as the means of getting a better one, and use your present enviornment as the means of getting into a better one. Your vision of the right business, if held with faith and purpose, will cause the Supreme to move the right business toward you; and your action, if performed in the Certain Way, will cause you to move toward the business.

If you are an employee, or wage earner, and feel that you must change places in order to get what you want, do not 'project" your thought into space and rely upon it to get you another job. It will probably fail to do so.

Hold the vision of yourself in the job you want, while you ACT with faith and purpose on the job you have, and you will certainly get the job you want.

Your vision and faith will set the creative force in motion to bring it toward you, and your action will cause the forces in your own environment to move you toward the place you want. In closing this chapter, we will add another statement to our syllabus:

There is a thinking stuff from which all things are made, and which, in its original state, permeates, penetrates, and fills the interspaces of the universe.

A thought, in this substance, Produces the thing that is imaged by the thought.

Man can form things in his thought, and, by impressing his thought upon formless substance, can cause the thing he thinks about to be created.

In order to do this, man must pass from the competitive

to the creative mind; he must form a clear mental picture of the things he wants, and hold this picture in his thoughts with the fixed PURPOSE to get what he wants, and the unwavering FAITH that he does get what he wants, closing his mind to all that may tend to shake his purpose, dim his vision, or quench his faith.

That he may receive what he wants when it comes, man must act NOW upon the people and things in his present environment.

CHAPTER 12

Efficient Action

YOU must use your thought as directed in previous chapters, and begin to do what you can do where you are; and you must do ALL that you can do where you are.

You can advance only be being larger than your present place; and no man is larger than his present place who leaves undone any of the work pertaining to that place.

The world is advanced only by those who more than fill their present places.

If no man quite filled his present place, you can see that there must be a going backward in everything. Those who do not quite fill their present places are dead weight upon society, government, commerce, and industry; they must be carried along by others at a great expense. The progress of the world is retarded only by those who do not fill the places they are holding; they belong to a former age and a lower stage or plane of life, and their tendency is toward degeneration. No society could advance if every man was smaller than his place; social evolution is guided by the law of physical and mental evolution. In the animal world, evolution is caused by excess of life.

When an organism has more life than can be expressed in the functions of its own plane, it develops the organs of a higher plane, and a new species is originated.

There never would have been new species had there not been organisms which more than filled their places. The law is exactly the same for you; your getting rich depends upon your applying this principle to your own affairs.

Every day is either a successful day or a day of failure; and it is the successful days which get you what you want. If everyday is a failure, you can never get rich; while if every day is a success, you cannot fail to get rich.

If there is something that may be done today, and you do not do it, you have failed in so far as that thing is concerned; and the consequences may be more disastrous than you imagine.

You cannot foresee the results of even the most trivial act;

you do not know the workings of all the forces that have been set moving in your behalf. Much may be depending on your doing some simple act; it may be the very thing which is to open the door of opportunity to very great possibilities. You can never know all the combinations which Supreme Intelligence is making for you in the world of things and of human affairs; your neglect or failure to do some small thing may cause a long delay in getting what you want.

Do, every day, ALL that can be done that day.

There is, however, a limitation or qualification of the above that you must take into account.

You are not to overwork, nor to rush blindly into your business in the effort to do the greatest possible number of things in the shortest possible time.

You are not to try to do tomorrow's work today, nor to do a week's work in a day.

It is really not the number of things you do, but the EFFICIENCY of each separate action that counts.

Every act is, in itself, either a success or a failure.

Every act is, in itself, either effective or inefficient.

Every inefficient act is a failure, and if you spend your life in doing inefficient acts, your whole life will be a failure.

The more things you do, the worse for you, if all your acts are inefficient ones.

On the other hand, every efficient act is a success in itself, and if every act of your life is an efficient one, your whole life MUST be a success.

The cause of failure is doing too many things in an inefficient manner, and not doing enough things in an efficient manner.

You will see that it is a self-evident proposition that if you do not do any inefficient acts, and if you do a sufficient number of efficient acts, you will become rich. If, now, it is possible for you to make each act an efficient one, you see again that the getting of riches is reduced to an exact science, like mathematics.

The matter turns, then, on the questions whether you can make each separate act a success in itself. And this you can certainly do.

You can make each act a success, because ALL Power is

working with you; and ALL Power cannot fail.

Power is at your service; and to make each act efficient you have only to put power into it.

Every action is either strong or weak; and when every one is strong, you are acting in the Certain Way which will make you rich.

Every act can be made strong and efficient by holding your vision while you are doing it, and putting the whole power of your FAITH and PURPOSE into it.

It is at this point that the people fail who separate mental power from personal action. They use the power of mind in one place and at one time, and they act in another place and at another time. So their acts are not successful in themselves; too many of them are inefficient. But if ALL Power goes into every act, no matter how commonplace, every act will be a success in itself; and as in the nature of things every success opens the way to other successes, your progress toward what you want, and the progress of what you want toward you, will become increasingly rapid.

Remember that successful action is cumulative in its results. Since the desire for more life is inherent in all things, when a man begins to move toward larger life more things attach themselves to him, and the influence of his desire is multiplied.

Do, every day, all that you can do that day, and do each act in an efficient manner.

In saying that you must hold your vision while you are doing each act, however trivial or commonplace, I do not mean to say that it is necessary at all times to see the vision distinctly to its smallest details. It should be the work of your leisure hours to use your imagination on the details of your vision, and to contemplate them until they are firmly fixed upon memory. If you wish speedy results, spend practically all your spare time in this practice.

By continuous contemplation you will get the picture of what you want, even to the smallest details, so firmly fixed upon your mind, and so completely transferred to the mind of Formless Substance, that in your working hours you need only to mentally refer to the picture to stimulate your faith and purpose, and cause your best effort to be put forth. Contemplate your picture in your leisure hours until your consciousness is so full of it that you can grasp it instantly. You will become so enthused with its bright promises that the mere thought of it will call forth the strongest energies of your whole being.

Let us again repeat our syllabus, and by slightly changing the closing statements bring it to the point we have now reached.

There is a thinking stuff from which all things are made, and which, in its original state, permeates, penetrates, and fills the interspaces of the universe.

A thought, in this substance, Produces the thing that is imaged by the thought.

Man can form things in his thought, and, by impressing his thought upon formless substance, can cause the thing he thinks about to be created.

In order to do this, man must pass from the competitive to the creative mind; he must form a clear mental picture of the things he wants, and do, with faith and purpose, all that can be done each day, doing each separate thing in an efficient manner.

CHAPTER 13

Getting into the Right Business

SUCCESS, in any particular business, depends for one thing upon your possessing in a well-developed state the faculties required in that business.

Without good musical faculty no one can succeed as a teacher of music; without well-developed mechanical faculties no one can achieve great success in any of the mechanical trades; without tact and the commercial faculties no one can succeed in mercantile pursuits. But to possess in a well-developed state the faculties required in your particular vocation does not insure getting rich. There are musicians who have remarkable talent, and who yet remain poor; there are blacksmiths, carpenters, and so on who have excellent mechanical ability, but who do not get rich; and there are merchants with good faculties for dealing with men who nevertheless fail.

The different faculties are tools; it is essential to have good tools, but it is also essential that the tools should be used in the Right Way. One man can take a sharp saw, a square, a good plane, and so on, and build a handsome article of furniture; another man can take the same tools and set to work to duplicate the article, but his production will be a botch. He does not know how to use good tools in a successful way.

The various faculties of your mind are the tools with which you must do the work which is to make you rich; it will be easier for you to succeed if you get into a business for which you are well equipped with mental tools.

Generally speaking, you will do best in that business which will use your strongest faculties; the one for which you are naturally "best fitted." But there are limitations to this statement, also. No man should regard his vocation as being irrevocably fixed by the tendencies with which he was born.

You can get rich in ANY business, for if you have not the right talent for you can develop that talent; it merely means that you will have to make your tools as you go along, instead of confining yourself to the use of those with which you were born. It will be EASIER for you to succeed in a vocation for which you already have the talents in a well-developed state; but you CAN succeed in any vocation, for you can develop any rudimentary talent, and there is no talent of which you have not at least the rudiment.

You will get rich most easily in point of effort, if you do that for which you are best fitted; but you will get rich most satisfactorily if you do that which you WANT to do.

Doing what you want to do is life; and there is no real satisfaction in living if we are compelled to be forever doing something which we do not like to do, and can never do what we want to do. And it is certain that you can do what you want to do; the desire to do it is proof that you have within you the power which can do it.

Desire is a manifestation of power.

The desire to play music is the power which can play music seeking expression and development; the desire to invent mechanical devices is the mechanical talent seeking expression and development.

Where there is no power, either developed or undeveloped, to do a thing, there is never any desire to do that thing; and where there is strong desire to do a thing, it is certain proof that the power to do it is strong, and only requires to be developed and applied in the Right Way.

All things else being equal, it is best to select the business for which you have the best developed talent; but if you have a strong desire to engage in any particular line of work, you should select that work as the ultimate end at which you aim.

You can do what you want to do, and it is your right and privilege to follow the business or avocation which will be most congenial and pleasant.

You are not obliged to do what you do not like to do, and should not do it except as a means to bring you to the doing of the thing you want to do.

If there are past mistakes whose consequences have placed you in an undesirable business or environment, you may be obliged for some time to do what you do not like to do; but you can make the doing of it pleasant by knowing that it is making it possible for you to come to the doing of what you want to do.

If you feel that you are not in the right vocation, do not act too hastily in trying to get into another one. The best way, generally, to change business or environment is by growth.

Do not be afraid to make a sudden and radical change if the opportunity is presented, and you feel after careful consideration that it is the right opportunity; but never take sudden or radical action when you are in doubt as to the wisdom of doing so.

There is never any hurry on the creative plane; and there is no lack of opportunity.

When you get out of the competitive mind you will understand that you never need to act hastily. No one else is going to beat you to the thing you want to do; there is enough for all. If one space is taken, another and a better one will be opened for you a little farther on; there is plenty of time. When you are in doubt, wait. Fall back on the contemplation of your vision, and increase your faith and purpose; and by all means, in times of doubt and indecision, cultivate gratitude.

A day or two spent in contemplating the vision of what you want, and in earnest thanksgiving that you are getting it, will bring your mind into such close relationship with the Supreme that you will make no mistake when you do act.

There is a mind which knows all there is to know; and you can come into close unity with this mind by faith and the purpose to advance in life, if you have deep gratitude.

Mistakes come from acting hastily, or from acting in fear or doubt, or in forgetfulness of the Right Motive, which is more life to all, and less to none.

As you go on in the Certain Way, opportunities will come to you in increasing number; and you will need to be very steady in your faith and purpose, and to keep in close touch with the All Mind by reverent gratitude.

Do all that you can do in a perfect manner every day, but do it without haste, worry, or fear. Go as fast as you can, but never hurry.

Remember that in the moment you begin to hurry you cease to be a creator and become a competitor; you drop back upon the old plane again.

Whenever you find yourself hurrying, call a halt; fix your attention on the mental image of the thing you want, and begin to give thanks that you are getting it. The exercise of GRATITUDE will never fail to strengthen your faith and renew your purpose.

CHAPTER 14

The Impression of Increase

WHETHER you change your vocation or not, your actions for the present must be those pertaining to the business in which you are now engaged.

You can get into the business you want by making constructive use of the business you are already established in; by doing your daily work in a Certain Way.

And in so far as your business consists in dealing with other men, whether personally or by letter, the key-thought of all your efforts must be to convey to their minds the impression of increase.

Increase is what all men and all women are seeking; it is the urge of the Formless Intelligence within them, seeking fuller expression.

The desire for increase is inherent in all nature; it is the fundamental impulse of the universe. All human activities are based on the desire for increase; people are seeking more food, more clothes, better shelter, more luxury, more beauty, more knowledge, more pleasure—increase in something, more life.

Every living thing is under this necessity for continuous advancement; where increase of life ceases, dissolution and death set in at once.

Man instinctively knows this, and hence he is forever seeking more. This law of perpetual increase is set forth by Jesus in the parable of the talents; only those who gain more retain any; from him who hath not shall be taken away even that which he hath.

The normal desire for increased wealth is not an evil or a reprehensible thing; it is simply the desire for more abundant life; it is aspiration.

And because it is the deepest instinct of their natures, all men and women are attracted to him who can give them more of the means of life.

In following the Certain Way as described in the foregoing pages, you are getting continuous increase for yourself, and you are giving it to all with whom you deal.

You are a creative center, from which increase is given off to all.

Be sure of this, and convey assurance of the fact to every man, woman, and child with whom you come in contact. No matter how small the transaction, even if it be only the selling of a stick of candy to a little child, put into it the thought of increase, and make sure that the customer is impressed with the thought.

Convey the impression of advancement with everything you do, so that all people shall receive the impression that you are an Advancing Man, and that you advance all who deal with you. Even to the people whom you meet in a social way, without any thought of business, and to whom you do not try to sell anything, give the thought of increase.

You can convey this impression by holding the unshakable faith that you, yourself, are in the Way of Increase; and by letting this faith inspire, fill, and permeate every action.

Do everything that you do in the firm conviction that you are an advancing personality, and that you are giving advancement to everybody.

Feel that you are getting rich, and that in so doing you are making others rich, and conferring benefits on all.

Do not boast or brag of your success, or talk about it unnecessarily; true faith is never boastful.

Wherever you find a boastful person, you find one who is secretly doubtful and afraid. Simply feel the faith, and let it work out in every transaction; let every act and tone and look express the quiet assurance that you are getting rich; that you are already rich. Words will not be necessary to communicate this feeling to others; they will feel the sense of increase when in your presence, and will be attracted to you again.

You must so impress others that they will feel that in associating with you they will get increase for themselves. See that you give them a use value greater than the cash value you are taking from them.

Take an honest pride in doing this, and let everybody know it; and you will have no lack of customers. People will go where they are given increase; and the Supreme, which desires increase in all, and which knows all, will move toward you men and women who have never heard of you. Your business will increase rapidly, and you will be surprised at the unexpected benefits which will come to you. You will be able from day to day to make larger combinations, secure greater advantages, and to go on into a more congenial vocation if you desire to do so.

But doing thing all this, you must never lose sight of your vision of what you want, or your faith and purpose to get what you want.

Let me here give you another word of caution in regard to motives.

Beware of the insidious temptation to seek for power over other men.

Nothing is so pleasant to the unformed or partially developed mind as the exercise of power or dominion over others. The desire to rule for selfish gratification has been the curse of the world. For countless ages kings and lords have drenched the earth with blood in their battles to extend their dominions; this not to seek more life for all, but to get more power for themselves.

To-day, the main motive in the business and industrial world is the same; men marshal their armies of dollars, and lay waste the lives and hearts of millions in the same mad scramble for power over others. Commercial kings, like political kings, are inspired by the lust for power.

Jesus saw in this desire for mastery the moving impulse of that evil world He sought to overthrow. Read the twenty-third chapter of Matthew, and see how He pictures the lust of the Pharisees to be called "Master," to sit in the high places, to domineer over others, and to lay burdens on the backs of the less fortunate; and note how He compares this lust for dominion with the brotherly seeking for the Common Good to which He calls His disciples.

Look out for the temptation to seek for authority, to become a "master," to be considered as one who is above the common herd, to impress others by lavish display, and so on.

The mind that seeks for mastery over others is the competitive mind; and the competitive mind is not the creative one. In order to master your environment and your destiny, it is not at all necessary that you should rule over your fellow men and indeed, when you fall into the world's struggle for the high places, you begin to be conquered by fate and environment, and your getting rich becomes a matter of chance and speculation.

Beware of the competitive mind!! No better statement of the principle of creative action can be formulated than the favorite declaration of the late "Golden Rule" Jones of Toledo: "What I want for myself, I want for everybody."

CHAPTER 15

The Advancing Man

WHAT I have said in the last chapter applies as well to the professional man and the wage-earner as to the man who is engaged in mercantile business.

No matter whether you are a physician, a teacher, or a clergyman, if you can give increase of life to others and make them sensible of the fact, they will be attracted to you, and you will get rich. The physician who holds the vision of himself as a great and successful healer, and who works toward the complete realization of that vision with faith and purpose, as described in former chapters, will come into such close touch with the Source of Life that he will be phenomenally successful; patients will come to him in throngs.

No one has a greater opportunity to carry into effect the teaching of this book than the practitioner of medicine; it does not matter to which of the various schools he may belong, for the principle of healing is common to all of them, and may be reached by all alike. The Advancing Man in medicine, who holds to a clear mental image of himself as successful, and who obeys the laws of faith, purpose, and gratitude, will cure every curable case he undertakes, no matter what remedies he may use.

In the field of religion, the world cries out for the clergyman who can teach his hearers the true science of abundant life. He who masters the details of the science of getting rich, together with the allied sciences of being well, of being great, and of winning love, and who teaches these details from the pulpit, will never lack for a congregation. This is the gospel that the world needs; it will give increase of life, and men will hear it gladly, and will give liberal support to the man who brings it to them.

What is now needed is a demonstration of the science of life from the pulpit. We want preachers who can not only tell us how, but who in their own persons will show us how. We need the preacher who will himself be rich, healthy, great, and beloved, to teach us how to attain to these things; and when he comes he will find a numerous and loyal following.

The same is true of the teacher who can inspire the children with the faith and purpose of the advancing life. He will never be "out of a job." And any teacher who has this faith and purpose can give it to his pupils; he cannot help giving it to them if it is part of his own life and practice.

What is true of the teacher, preacher, and physician is true of the lawyer, dentist, real estate man, insurance agent—of everybody.

The combined mental and personal action I have described is infallible; it cannot fail. Every man and woman who follows these instructions steadily, perseveringly, and to the letter, will get rich. The law of the Increase of Life is as mathematically certain in its operation as the law of gravitation; getting rich is an exact science.

The wage-earner will find this as true of his case as of any of the others mentioned. Do not feel that you have no chance to get rich because you are working where there is no visible opportunity for advancement, where wages are small and the cost of living high. Form your clear mental vision of what you want, and begin to act with faith and purpose.

Do all the work you can do, every day, and do each piece of work in a perfectly successful manner; put the power of success, and the purpose to get rich, into everything that you do.

But do not do this merely with the idea of currying favor with your employer, in the hope that he, or those above you, will see your good work and advance you; it is not likely that they will do so.

The man who is merely a "good" workman, filling his place to the very best of his ability, and satisfied with that, is valuable to his employer; and it is not to the employer's interest to promote him; he is worth more where he is.

To secure advancement, something more is necessary than to be too large for your place.

The man who is certain to advance is the one who is too big for his place, and who has a clear concept of what he wants to be; who knows that he can become what he wants to be and who is determined to BE what he wants to be.

Do not try to more than fill your present place with a view to pleasing your employer; do it with the idea of advancing yourself. Hold the faith and purpose of increase during work hours, after work hours, and before work hours. Hold it in such a way that every person who comes in contact with you, whether foreman, fellow workman, or social acquaintance, will feel the power of purpose radiating from you; so that every one will get the sense of advancement and increase from you. Men will be attracted to you, and if there is no possibility for advancement in your present job, you will very soon see an opportunity to take another job.

There is a Power which never fails to present opportunity to the Advancing Man who is moving in obedience to law.

God cannot help helping you, if you act in a Certain Way; He must do so in order to help Himself.

There is nothing in your circumstances or in the industrial situation that can keep you down. If you cannot get rich working for the steel trust, you can get rich on a ten-acre farm; and if you begin to move in the Certain Way, you will certainly escape from the "clutches" of the steel trust and get on to the farm or wherever else you wish to be.

If a few thousands of its employees would enter upon the Certain Way, the steel trust would soon be in a bad plight; it would have to give its workingmen more opportunity, or go out of business. Nobody has to work for a trust; the trusts can keep men in so called hopeless conditions only so long as there are men who are too ignorant to know of the science of getting rich, or too intellectually slothful to practice it.

Begin this way of thinking and acting, and your faith and purpose will make you quick to see any opportunity to better your condition.

Such opportunities will speedily come, for the Supreme, working in All, and working for you, will bring them before you.

Do not wait for an opportunity to be all that you want to be; when an opportunity to be more than you are now is presented and you feel impelled toward it, take it. It will be the first step toward a greater opportunity.

There is no such thing possible in this universe as a lack of opportunities for the man who is living the advancing life.

It is inherent in the constitution of the cosmos that all things shall be for him and work together for his good; and he must certainly get rich if he acts and thinks in the Certain Way. So let wage-earning men and women study this book with great care, and enter with confidence upon the course of action it prescribes; it will not fail.

CHAPTER 16

Some Cautions, and Concluding Observations

MANY people will scoff at the idea that there is an exact science of getting rich; holding the impression that the supply of wealth is limited, they will insist that social and governmental institutions must be changed before even any considerable number of people can acquire a competence.

But this is not true.

It is true that existing governments keep the masses in poverty, but this is because the masses do not think and act in the Certain Way.

If the masses begin to move forward as suggested in this book, neither governments nor industrial systems can check them; all systems must be modified to accommodate the forward movement.

If the people have the Advancing Mind, have the Faith that they can become rich, and move forward with the fixed purpose to become rich, nothing can possibly keep them in poverty.

Individuals may enter upon the Certain Way at any time, and under any government, and make themselves rich; and when any considerable number of individuals do so under any government, they will cause the system to be so modified as to open the way for others.

The more men who get rich on the competitive plane, the worse for others; the more who get rich on the creative plane, the better for others.

The economic salvation of the masses can only be accomplished by getting a large number of people to practice the scientific method set down in this book, and become rich. These will show others the way, and inspire them with a desire for real life, with the faith that it can be attained, and with the purpose to attain it.

For the present, however, it is enough to know that neither the government under which you live nor the capitalistic or competitive system of industry can keep you from getting rich. When you enter upon the creative plane of thought you will rise above all these things and become a citizen of another kingdom.

But remember that your thought must be held upon the

creative plane; you are never for an instant to be betrayed into regarding the supply as limited, or into acting on the moral level of competition.

Whenever you do fall into old ways of thought, correct yourself instantly; for when you are in the competitive mind, you have lost the cooperation of the Mind of the Whole.

Do not spend any time in planning as to how you will meet possible emergencies in the future, except as the necessary policies may affect your actions today. You are concerned with doing today's work in a perfectly successful manner, and not with emergencies which may arise tomorrow; you can attend to them as they come.

Do not concern yourself with questions as to how you shall surmount obstacles which may loom upon your business horizon, unless you can see plainly that your course must be altered today in order to avoid them.

No matter how tremendous an obstruction may appear at a distance, you will find that if you go on in the Certain Way it will disappear as you approach it, or that a way over, though, or around it will appear.

No possible combination of circumstances can defeat a man or woman who is proceeding to get rich along strictly scientific lines. No man or woman who obeys the law can fail to get rich, any more than one can multiply two by two and fail to get four.

Give no anxious thought to possible disasters, obstacles, panics, or unfavorable combinations of circumstances; it is time enough to meet such things when they present themselves before you in the immediate present, and you will find that every difficulty carries with it the wherewithal for its overcoming.

Guard your speech. Never speak of yourself, your affairs, or of anything else in a discouraged or discouraging way.

Never admit the possibility of failure, or speak in a way that infers failure as a possibility.

Never speak of the times as being hard, or of business conditions as being doubtful. Times may be hard and business doubtful for those who are on the competitive plane, but they can never be so for you; you can create what you want, and you are above fear.

When others are having hard times and poor business, you will find your greatest opportunities.

Train yourself to think of and to look upon the world as a something which is Becoming, which is growing; and to regard seeming evil as being only that which is undeveloped. Always speak in terms of advancement; to do otherwise is to deny your faith, and to deny your faith is to lose it.

Never allow yourself to feel disappointed. You may expect to have a certain thing at a certain time, and not get it at that time; and this will appear to you like failure.

But if you hold to your faith you will find that the failure is only apparent.

Go on in the certain way, and if you do not receive that thing, you will receive something so much better that you will see that the seeming failure was really a great success.

A student of this science had set his mind on making a certain business combination which seemed to him at the time to be very desirable, and he worked for some, weeks to bring it about. When the crucial time came, the thing failed in a perfectly inexplicable way; it was as if some unseen influence had been working secretly against him. He was not disappointed; on the contrary, he thanked God that his desire had been overruled, and went steadily on with a grateful mind. In a few weeks an opportunity so much better came his way that he would not have made the first deal on any account; and he saw that a Mind which knew more than he knew had prevented him from losing the greater good by entangling himself with the lesser.

That is the way every seeming failure will work out for you, if you keep your faith, hold to your purpose, have gratitude, and do, every day, all that can be done that day, doing each separate act in a successful manner.

When you make a failure, it is because you have not asked for enough; keep on, and a larger thing then you were seeking will certainly come to you. Remember this.

You will not fail because you lack the necessary talent to do what you wish to do. If you go on as I have directed, you will develop all the talent that is necessary to the doing of your work.

It is not within the scope of this book to deal with the science of cultivating talent; but it is as certain and simple as the process of getting rich.

However, do not hesitate or waver for fear that when you come to any certain place you will fail for lack of ability; keep right on, and when you come to that place, the ability will be furnished to you. The same source of Ability which enabled the untaught Lincoln to do the greatest work in government ever accomplished by a single man is open to you; you may draw upon all the mind there is for wisdom to use in meeting the responsibilities which are laid upon you. Go on in full faith.

Study this book. Make it your constant companion until you have mastered all the ideas contained in it. While you are getting firmly established in this faith, you will do well to give up most recreations and pleasure; and to stay away from places where ideas conflicting with these are advanced in lectures or sermons. Do not read pessimistic or conflicting literature, or get into arguments upon the matter. Do very little reading, outside of the writers mentioned in the Preface. Spend most of your leisure time in contemplating your vision, and in cultivating gratitude, and in reading this book. It contains all you need to know of the science of getting rich; and you will find all the essentials summed up in the following chapter.

CHAPTER 17

Summary of *The Science of Getting Rich*

THERE is a thinking stuff from which all things are made, and which, in its original state, permeates, penetrates, and fills the interspaces of the universe.

A thought in this substance produces the thing that is imaged by the thought.

Man can form things in his thought, and by impressing his thought upon formless substance can cause the thing he thinks about to be created.

In order to do this, man must pass from the competitive to the creative mind; otherwise he cannot be in harmony with the Formless Intelligence, which is always creative and never competitive in spirit.

Man may come into full harmony with the Formless Substance by entertaining a lively and sincere gratitude for the blessings it bestows upon him. Gratitude unifies the mind of man with the intelligence of Substance, so that man's thoughts are received by the Formless. Man can remain upon the creative plane only by uniting himself with the Formless Intelligence through a deep and continuous feeling of gratitude .

Man must form a clear and definite mental image of the things he wishes to have, to do, or to become; and he must hold this mental image in his thoughts, while being deeply grateful to the Supreme that all his desires are granted to him. The man who wishes to get rich must spend his leisure hours in contemplating his Vision, and in earnest thanksgiving that the reality is being given to him. Too much stress cannot be laid on the importance of frequent contemplation of the mental image, coupled with unwavering faith and devout gratitude. This is the process by which the impression is given to the Formless, and the creative forces set in motion.

The creative energy works through the established channels of natural growth, and of the industrial and social order. All that is included in his mental image will surely be brought to the man who follows the instructions given above, and whose faith does not waver. What he wants will come to him through the ways of established trade and commerce.

In order to receive his own when it shall come to him, man must be active; and this activity can only consist in more than filling his present place. He must keep in mind the Purpose to get rich through the realization of his mental image. And he must do, every day, all that can be done that day, taking care to do each act in a successful manner. He must give to every man a use value in excess of the cash value he receives, so that each transaction makes for more life; and he must so hold the Advancing Thought that the impression of increase will be communicated to all with whom he comes in contact.

The men and women who practice the foregoing instructions will certainly get rich; and the riches they receive will be in exact proportion to the definiteness of their vision, the fixity of their purpose, the steadiness of their faith, and the depth of their gratitude.

The End

INDEX

C

M

T

BEYOND THE BLEEP: The Definitive Unauthorized Guide to *What the Bleep Do We Know!?*

By Alexandra Bruce

An essential guide to the hit new age film which plunges you into a world where everything is alive, and reality is changed by every thought.

This book illuminates the personalities and teachings of the physicists, physicians, spiritual teachers, mystics and scholars in the film *What the Bleep Do We Know!?*, helping the reader sort through their wilder theories with simple explanations of the cutting-edge science on which they are based. There is a huge demand for more information on the topics presented in the film; *Beyond the Bleep* is the place to start.

Spirituality / Science • Trade Paperback • 288 pages
$9.95 • ISBN: 978-1932857-22-1

ABOUT THE AUTHOR

Alexandra Bruce's articles on urban legends, metaphysical and quantum physics themes have been published in Paranoia Magazine, Steamshovel Press, Borderland Sciences and Disinfo.com. She has translated the book *Celestial Secrets, The Hidden History of the Mystery of Fátima* with a foreword by Jim Marrs, and is the author of *Beyond The Bleep: The Definitive Unauthorized Guide to What the Bleep Do We Know!?*. She lives in Rio de Janeiro and Southampton, New York.